C000059327

EXCELLENCE IN MINISTRY

A Guide to Protocols and Etiquette for Church Leaders

BY: Dr. O. J. SHABAZZ

Excellence in Ministry

A Guide to Protocols and Etiquettes for
Church Leaders

By: Dr. O. J. Shabazz

EXCELLENCE in Ministry

© 2023 Dr. O. J. Shabazz

All rights reserved. No part of this book may be reproduced, stored in a retrieval system, or transmitted in any form or by any means without the prior written permission of the publisher, except by a reviewer who may quote brief passages in a review to be printed in a newspaper, magazine or journal.

You can contact me for copies and other pertinent concerns at:

DrOJShabazz@msn.com

ISBN: 979-8-218-23336-5

Table Of Contents

O.J. **SHABAZZ**
MINISTRIES

Foreword

The term *Excellence* is often used and means different things to different people. At any rate, in its simplest form, most would agree that excellence is the quality of being outstanding or extremely good. It means being great or the best at something, yet achieving excellence is never easy. Excellence is also a quality that people really appreciate but is often hard to find. However, this is certainly not the case with the author of this volume.

A national and internationally recognized minister of the Gospel for more than four decades, a supportive husband and father, as well as a community activist, Olu Shabazz has allowed God to use him to perfect what I believe is a *must-have* volume among those who are Christian ministers, preachers, and teachers of the Gospel. This is especially a resource for those preaching and teaching in an organized congregation, be it in person or virtual.

Excellence in Ministry contains important tenets a minister of the Gospel needs to know to be the best that they can be and to do the best they can do to reflect the moral virtue and strive toward what is positive, valuable, and praiseworthy. Shabazz reminds us of what Timothy 3:1-10 points out, that is, God has expectations and requirements for those who pursue positions of leadership within the church. It is not a role that should be taken lightly because it comes with influence and significant responsibility. Church leaders must hold themselves to a higher standard.

Although God expects all Christians to strive toward perfection, whether we like it or not, ministers, preachers and teachers of the Gospel are often held to a higher standard among those they lead or serve. Shabazz says this is because they are first and foremost "servants," and as the Word of God says in Matthew 23:11, "The greatest among us are servants."

Since Matthew 28:19-20 makes it clear that those who are members of the Body of Jesus Christ are compelled to, "Go into the world and preach and teach the Gospel that others might be saved," Shabazz writes from a position of experience that clearly points out that God is the standard against which everything is measured. Though written to ministers of the Gospel, this volume is applicable to every Christian since all of us are called to carry out God's command to preach, teach and reach the lost.

The wisdom God instilled in Olu Shabazz is eloquently displayed in this volume. The book enlightens, provides sound counsel and proven examples that should strengthen those preaching, and it should nourish and enrich their recipients. The volume is unique, inspiring, infallible and full of relevant examples of what one should do to administer and manage a local congregation. The examples are relevant and will lead to the practical ministerial etiquette that Shabazz purports.

New preachers/ministers, as well as seasoned ones, will find the chapters on fundamentals, following and serving under a retired preacher, delegating duties and responsibilities, as well as administering different ministries to be of immense value and easy to emulate. This is especially important as one leads in a post Covid-19 environment in which in-person or online church ministries may continue to bring about unique challenges and opportunities.

Robert R. Jennings, Ed. D., MBA 10th President, Alabama A&M University & 13th President, Lincoln University of PA

Acknowledgments

In the work, *Excellence in Ministry: Protocols and Etiquettes for Church Leaders,* Dr. Olu J. Shabazz has gifted preachers and church Leaders with a once in a generation mandatory read for those graced with the opportunity to be involved in ministry.

The work is enriched by stories reflecting his years of practical experience, his insight into the biblical text, and his engagement with contemporary scholarship. The work meets the standard of excellence it encourages for nearly every aspect of ministry.

Whether persons are new or experienced in ministry, this work will be a welcome guide for knowledge and growth. There is no other work comparable.

Dr. Jefferson R. Caruthers Jr.

Dr. Olu Shabazz has covered the full spectrum of ministerial excellence in the world on ministry laying the essential fingerprints of etiquette within this divine profession. Methodically laying forth a foundational understanding of ethics and practically providing a road map to ministry development, this book is a must-have for those who lead ministry.

Dr. Orpheus Heyward

When Edward Kennedy was challenging Jimmy Carter for the presidency in 1979, Carter, struggling in the polls, was entangled in a series of international problems, repeatedly accusing the president of "lurching from crisis to crisis."

That phrase bothered me because, whether the charge pertained to Carter or not, I felt it applied to me. My ministry lunged from one headache to another. I spent too much time putting out fires and too little time fanning the flames of the Spirit. I neither had a long-range plan for my work nor any system for developing one. Preachers as well as presidents can lurch from crisis to crisis and from day to day. Sometimes we lurch from church to church.

Weak leadership merely reacts to its ever-changing circumstances. Wiser leadership charts a course, follows its plan, and responds to the variables accordingly. Feeble leaders are crisis driven, while stronger ones are goal-directed. Prudent preachers do not just minister-they *ad*minister. In seminary, I learned more about alliteration than administration. In this important work, Dr. Shabazz has chartered a course and provided an excellent tool to help the busy preacher to administrate effectiveness in the Kingdom of God.

Solomon said, "a prudent man gives thought to his steps" (Proverbs 14:15 NIV). If we fail to plan, we plan to fail. Dr. Shabazz is helping us to succeed by providing practical wisdom for us to follow.

Dr. Richard L. Barclay

Stonecrest Church of Christ

McDonough, Georgia

It is with resounding appreciation for this work which is long overdue and it cannot be but beneficial not only to aspiring evangelist but as well as for those who are on the battlefield! I highly commend Dr. Shabazz for his in sight-fullness, clarity of thought, the conceptual of articulation and the forthright attitude demonstrated in these beneficial gold nuggets of practicality and years of ministerial wisdom. I commend it to all!

Luis R. Lugo

"The more things change the more they stay the same." While I do not know who first coined this familiar phrase, it expresses a well-established truth that applies to most things. This truth is echoed in the words of King Solomon, *"The thing that hath been, it is that which shall be; and that which is done is that which shall be done: and there is no new thing under the sun (Ecclesiastes 1:9).* There is a reliable consistency in life. Interestingly, this truth is in several ways applicable to the author of this book, ***Excellence in Ministry,*** making the book a valuable guide, regarding proper protocols and etiquettes in church leadership.

For Dr. Olu the words, ***Protocol and Etiquette*** are perfect terms that summarize an important aspect of his character. There is a reliable consistency in his life that makes Dr. Shabazz uniquely qualified to offer this timely guide to those who wish to improve their service in the Lord's work. This is a must read and a needed guide for those who are determined to do "all things decently, and in order."

Martin E. Thomas, D.PC, MDiv
Founder and Executive Director
Foresight For-Givers Foundation & The Nazareth Man House

Dedications

With heartfelt gratitude and appreciation, I dedicate this book to the following influences upon my ministry and life.

First and foremost, I dedicate this book to my faithful, supportive, and encouraging wife, *L.V.R. Shabazz,* who has relentlessly pushed me over the years to put these practical ministerial experiences in a book with hopes that this will help others pursue excellence in life's laboratory of experiences.

She has been relentless that a book of this kind is needed by those who may require practical recommendations of best practices while traveling through life's journey.

I would also like to dedicate this book to one of my trusted friends, Dr. Anthony (Tony) Roach of the Minda Street Church of Christ in Abilene, Texas, who reassured me that I could write this book excellently and was convinced of the need for my experiences in ministry, that it might aide others.

Last, I dedicate this work to all preachers, ministers, evangelists, young and mature, teachers, elders, deacons, church ministry leaders, church administrators, families, and others in search of excellence to the honor and glory of God Almighty.

O. J. Shabazz D. Min

Introduction

In 1979, life took an unexpected turn for me. In the years of my younger life, I was reared under the influence of a good father who was a devout Muslim, as were all of his children in his house. After leaving my father's home, and establishing my own house of authority, intense studies of the Quran and the Bible became one of my life's focuses.

As a result of my study and research, I became convicted to become a New Testament Christian soon after I started on a God-guided journey to preach and teach the Gospel of Jesus Christ at the tender age of 25.

Over 42 years, it has been my good fortune to have preached the Gospel as a Minister, Preacher, and Teacher, in three congregations of the Lord's church, in the Mid-South, Mid-West, and North-East portions of the United States of America. Over that same period, I have traveled the world conducting lectures, workshops, Gospel Campaigns, seminars, and Gospel revivals in over 39 States, 95 Cities, and five Nations.

Early in ministry, I developed a passion for training others to preach, teach and work in the context of local and National Ministry. To date, I have mentored and developed 18 preachers of the Gospel of Jesus Christ, the majority of which is currently serving in some capacity in Kingdom works.

In 1982, while still working on a Bachelor's degree in Biblical Studies at the Memphis School of Preaching in Memphis, Tennessee, I discovered that I had been amply trained in Bible and related subjects yet knew little or nothing about church administration and management of difficult people and personalities, not to mention the untold components of ministry structure and organization.

At this point, I studied everything I could get my hands on to equip myself better to engage in church administration and ministry management matters. I became driven to accomplish all I could for the God of my salvation with excellence. I wanted to go above and beyond the normal to make the cause of Christ shine. After all, when we serve a big God, we ought to accomplish big things in a big way.

Over the years, several people have suggested that I sit down and put these many experiences in print. Therefore, this book is different from years of academic training. Still, the fruit of countless mountaintop and valley experiences garnered from having worked for the Lord in the context of the local church, traveling extensively around the world, and training gospel soldiers to do the work of God with excellence.

It is my prayer and desire that my experiences will in some way benefit those who desire to serve the people of God and the world at large with excellence as they carry the gospel of our Lord Jesus Christ. Therefore, after much introspection and deliberation, I determined to target this book toward Ministers or servants and others whom God may lead to serve in the context of local, national, and international ministry.

By the time one has completed the content of this book, one should have a deeper grasp of those matters that go into formulating practical ministerial etiquette and protocols driven by a need to accomplish them with excellence.

This book will start with a much-needed definitional perspective of keywords and concepts: Minister, Etiquette, Protocol, and Excellence. Then, I will present an introspective challenge for the minister who is determining if his ministry is one of purpose or personal choice.

The book provides a detailed understanding of the significant challenges facing the ministering servant as the preacher is led to one's first service work. How to engage the search process, how to view the search process, and considerations concerning the minister's contract or work agreement will be covered. The book also treats several suggested etiquettes and protocols relative to what ministers want to observe. It discusses matters that they want to avoid during the first years of a new ministry.

Another focus of the book is how to engage passive-aggressive leaders and the managing of difficult people. How does one handle situations when the previous minister is still around and perhaps now serves the church as a "minister emeritus?" Great emphasis will be placed on the notion of excellence instead of professionalism regarding the execution of ministry. Great energy will be given to avoid the ongoing debate surrounding man's need to enjoy titles such as minister, pastor, evangelist, bishop, and the like, as opposed to having a preverbal towel; godly men do not need labels to validate that they need towels to manifest their Kingdom labor.

Last, I would like to express my heartfelt appreciation to my loving and supportive wife, L.V.R. Shabazz, and one of my dearest friends, Dr. Tony Roach of Dallas, Texas, for constantly pushing me to put these experiences to print.

CHAPTER 1

Definitional Perspectives

Protocol

In excellent thinking framework suggests that a word, subject, theme, or topic, well defined, is already half taught. As a result, it would be most valuable to provide a definitional perspective of a few keywords and subsequent concepts embodied in the following chapters of this book. The first is what is meant by the term "Minister."

It has always been intriguing and exciting to listen to the constant, never-ending discussions surrounding the need and subsequent uses of titles in the church (such as minister, evangelist, elder, deacon, teacher, pastor, reverend, and missionary). For some strange reason, people feel empowered by using particular titles.

The Use of the Word Minister

Etiquette

This is not an attempt to offer a theological polemic in defense or rejecting titles. Several of these previous designations are very scriptural in nature. The scriptures are clear concerning the correct destinations for those who serve in the work and governance of the local church.

In the strictest biblical sense, a minister is nothing more or less than a servant. The word minister is used consistently throughout the New Testament in one form or another. In Vine's Expository Dictionary of the Old & New Testament, W. E. Vines says: "The word Minister in the noun form is from the Greek word "Diakonos" meaning a servant, attendant, minister. Deacon is translated as minister (Mark 10:43; Romans 13:4; 15:8. In the verb form, it is the Greek word "Diakoneo" akin to the noun form, which signifies to be a servant, attendant, to serve, wait upon, minister" (Matthew 4:11; 20:28; Mark 1:13; 10:45; John 12:26). (1)

Accordingly, the designation "Minister" is much more than a title; it describes one's work. To this end, a minister is not just what one is called, nor what one does, but who you are, a call to a life of service. Therefore, it is not a matter of debate that God intended a minister to be a worker, carrying out the great commission as recorded in (Matthew 28:19-20), giving oneself to a life of Christian service (Matthew 23:11).

As one views the Holy Scriptures with an open and honest mind, one may quickly agree that how a man of God should be referenced should not be relegated to a simple matter of titles. Instead, it is more clearly the need for having a preverbal towel or works. Towels belong to those who perspire; those who sweat engage in spiritual works.

Further, concerning the definitional perspective of "minister," allow me to advance the notion that the failed attempts of a few in the church to insert humanistic motivated

(1) Vine's Expository Dictionary of the Old & New Testament pg. 744 are without divine authority. A case in point would be using titles like 'Senior Minister,' a distinction foreign to the Holy Scriptures.

This subject is not at all absent from the Holy Scriptures, for time and again, our Lord discouraged the practice of human elevation for ego's sake.

On many occasions within the context of scripture, there were those called Ministers. For example, the Apostle Paul often referred to himself as a "Minister" (Colossians 1:23, 25; I Corinthians 3:5; II Corinthians 6:4). Other great servants of God were called "Ministers" within scripture, men like Apollos (I Corinthians 3:5), Tychicus

(Ephesians 6:21), Epaphras (Colossians 1:7), Timothy (I Thessalonians 3:2; I Timothy 4:6).

During the earthly ministry of our Lord Jesus Christ, did the Lord refer to Himself as a "Minister" (Mark 10:45)? The Apostle Paul reports that the Messiah was a "minister to both Jews and Gentiles" (Romans 15:8). It seems that it was a great honor to be identified as a "Minister" of the gospel of Jesus Christ.

Another instance of what appears to be an attempt to misuse biblical titles would be the traditional usage of the designation "Pastor," at least in the context of our Western culture, among many Afro-American Evangelical Churches, along with many Churches of Christ and several Restoration movement churches. The exciting thing about the usage of this designation is that it is never one time used in the singular form in the Greek text of the New Testament, at least not in the manner in which many are now attempting to use it, as though it were a synonym for "minister."

In the New Testament Bible, the word "Pastor" is translated from the Greek word "Poimen." Poimen occurs some 18 times, most frequently referring to Jesus. In most English translations of the New Testament Bible, "Poimen" is translated as "Pastors" once, "Shepherd"13 times, and "Shepherds" four times. Yet "Pastor" is never one time translated in the singular form.

On several occasions, the argument has been advanced that this is a destination drawn from the verb form, indicating a description of what one does.

This may be an excellent place to clearly, and with the utmost transparency, declare that in most Afro-American churches, much of the work undertaken by the minister constitutes "Pastoring." This, I would argue, without fear of successful contradiction. He preaches, teaches, counsels, oversees much, if not all, of the ministries of the local congregation, and the list goes on and on.

However, the question becomes, are we who and what we are based on what we do, or are we who and what we are based on what God calls us in the scripture? If we are who and what we are based on simply what we do, then a large number of members of local churches are far better "pastors" than a number of those who claim to be called to be "pastors." We must be content to be known by the destinations assigned by God and not the trends of human beings and church trends.

A Definitional Perspective

The Use of the Word Etiquette

The word "etiquette," according to Webster's New College Dictionary, means "the forms, manners, and ceremonies established by convention as acceptable or required in social relations, in a profession, or official life. The rules for such forms, manners, and ceremonies." (2) More simply put, it carries with it the idea of a customary code of behavior in a society or among members of a particular group.

Etiquettes may be written as well as unwritten. Etiquettes are designed to establish acceptable norms within a specific culture to interact with others. These become guidelines for handling oneself among a particular group in ministry.

Concerning ministers and other church servants and groups, the Bible is replete with principles, precepts, and practices, which may help establish ministry etiquettes. However, these etiquettes are not designed to violate any laws or commands taught by God in the Holy Scriptures.

The Bible does not just teach by positive and negative divine commands and approved scriptural examples. It also teaches necessary inferences when respected by the author's intent in writing. These are just a sample of many tested and tried hermeneutical principles, often called Pattern Theology or Pattern Authority. While this is not intended to be a lesson in hermeneutics, it is an approach to extracting any number of solid principles from the Word of God that may go into formulating ministry etiquettes.

(2) Webster's New College Dictionary pg. 48

Etiquettes are often developed as a matter of good common sense. It is a real down-to-earth, how-to best carry it out or get it done approach. However, do not ignore the idea that etiquette may need to be updated and changed occasionally. Circumstances may dictate the need to do things in a better way than previously done.

Look at good etiquette practices as a newly established body of policies you have opted to adapt to enjoy more excellent standards of excellence. There are two simple words that best describe etiquette; they are "the how." Therefore, much time should be invested into developing healthy approaches to effectively carrying out ministry etiquette. This is the gateway to ministry driven by excellence.

In the ministry world, there is much room for doing projects, programs, and hosted events, particularly in how they are executed. Nothing is more rewarding than hearing someone say, "I have never had this kind of experience before," or "This is a first for me." On one occasion, I invited a minister to be a guest speaker at an annual church revival. I drafted a detailed invitation letter with the day, date, and times of the revival and an agreement to cover his round-trip airfare from his city to ours and back.

The amount of stipend, the agreement to lift a love offering, the location of proposed housing, and a covenant to provide food for the time he was to be at the church were also included. We mailed him a travel per dim two weeks in advance of his coming to take care of clothing that may have needed to be cleaned before the trip, baggage fees while on the journey in, food for the trip in, and an offer to bring his wife along at the expense of the local church. The response I received was, "I have never seen this before."

These constituted a few simple etiquettes driven by a need to get it done with excellence. This became a standard of decorum for our congregation when hosting an event. Excellence, excellence, excellence, is the driving motivation.

A Definitional Perspective

The Use of the Word Protocol

The word "Protocol," in one definition, carries with it the idea of: "The established code of procedure or behavior in any group, organization, or situation." However, the protocol has several meanings, all connected to guidelines or procedures to follow. The most common purpose of the protocol is "a system of rules that explain the correct conduct and procedures to be followed in formal situations."

Today, there are many proper protocols, such as safety, academic, government, computer, and ministerial protocols. However, there is an ongoing debate about whether protocols have any place in the Christian system, let alone in the ministry world—the discussion in the negative needs to be improved. The Old and New Testaments are designed to be books of established behaviors for God-fearing people in the canon of scripture.

The books of First Timothy, Second Timothy, and Titus teach codes, behaviors, guidelines, procedures, and systems of rules that may be identified as Christian protocols. For this book, I will be treating the word "protocol" in the context of "what you do" as opposed to "how it's done." These protocols will seek to identify executable practices that have become recognized standards and norms in the ministry world.

The aim and motivation to utilize ministry protocols are to achieve the works of God driven by excellence. The God of the Holy Bible is a God of excellence. Even a cursory view of the Bible's God will reveal that He does nothing that does not constitute excellence.

Therefore, a minister will want to avoid that framework of thinking, "I'll do enough to get by." As we move forward, remember, as a framework of thinking, that every protocol implemented will be viewed as a matter of established practice, which will become your standard way of what you do, driven by excellence.

A Definitional Perspective

The Use of the Word Excellence

According to The Merriam-Webster Dictionary New Edition pg. 171"Excellence" means: "the quality of being excellent: an excellent or valuable quality: Virtue." The additive form of the word "excellent" means "very good of its kind: First-Class." (4)

The concept of excellence may be found throughout the Bible. In the Old Testament Bible, the Hebrew word for "Excellence" is the word "adder," meaning "great or honorable" (Psalm 8:1, 9; 16:3; 76:4). From the Aramaic word "yattir," meaning "surpassing, as seen in (Daniel 2:31; 4:36; 5:12, 14; 6:3). In the New Testament Bible, we have "diaphoroteros" meaning "greater," "better" (Hebrews 1:4; 8:6).

The very idea of excellence carries the idea of what is excellent, honorable, surpassing, better, or more significant. This is meant in our treatment and subsequent use of "excellence." Therefore, in all a minister undertakes, one should strive for better, more significant, or surpass what is considered normal.

The God we serve is a God of excellence. All He has created and done has always been done in the spirit of excellence. For the minister of God, his reach should always be for excellence as he endeavors to execute the words, ways, and will of the God of our salvation.

While in my early years of ministry, I pushed for professionalism, thinking this was an optimal goal to achieve and produce the best for a Kingdom agenda. As I studied the Bible more and more, I learned that the idea of professionalism was more of a secular concept; I learned to put away the notion of professionalism and replace it with something much better, "excellence."

All of the protocols and etiquettes developed within the context of ministry must be driven by the goal of getting it all done with excellence. The very notion of excellence is biblical, spiritual, and godly. It must become the optimal goal of every minister of the Gospel of Jesus Christ. We are to reach for the best, most excellent, and most honorable that we can give the Kingdom, the cause, and Christ.

(4) The Merriam-Webster Dictionary New Edition pg. 171

CHAPTER 2

Protocols, Etiquette, and Excellence Biblically

Protocol

Even the casual student of the Bible may easily see that the God we serve is a God of excellence. Everything God creates, says, does, plans, legislates, and executes, He does with unquestionable excellence. This means God Himself is the model to be studied when desiring a world of ministerial excellence. From the world's creation, as recorded in the early chapters of the book of Genesis (Genesis 1-2), to God's Revelation concerning man's scheme of redemption, every bit of it all constitutes sheer excellence.

An efficient and logical question is: "How can a church leader approach the development of needed protocols and etiquette to achieve excellence?" While reading the Bible, where and how should the church leader look for direction in developing protocol and etiquette? God Almighty is never wasteful; He never does something for nothing. As a result, He should be examined closely. Preacher, the Word of God, is the place to look for protocols and etiquette.

In this protocol, I want to point out several approaches that may assist a church leader in how to look for foundational concepts that can be transposed into church protocols and etiquette. Namely, the many patterns established by God in scripture,

His transparent practices, the principles that may be extracted from the sacred text, and the many precepts seen throughout the Word all serve as a tremendous foundational premise for church protocols and etiquette.

This is a far greater concept than professionalism, whose standards are established and followed by mere men. These are God's concepts, the designer of excellence, and an example worthy of following. So, for the remainder of this chapter, let us understand biblical patterns, practices, principles, and precepts that mold, shape and develop protocols and etiquette, which result in excellence.

Bible Patterns

Etiquette

In the world of theology, there is an interpretive process known as Pattern Authority or Pattern Theology. Pattern Theology examines the sacred text as you look for established patterns throughout scripture. One will pay attention to what was done, the number of times it was done, and how it was done. God is a God of the pattern. Leaders may use these patterns to establish traditional protocols and etiquette. This is not an attempt to develop some new and binding law. A leader never wants to bind laws that God did not bind. Nonetheless, a given pattern is often enough for a leader to develop a protocol or etiquette based on what has been seen in the Word of God. This makes the protocol and or etiquette Bible based.

Dating back to the Restoration era, many ascribed to the notion of God's patterns in scripture. The three components that undergirded pattern authority are positive and negative divine commands, approved scriptural examples, and necessary inferences. This may require additional research and understanding when an example is binding to interpret the pattern correctly. Nevertheless, the Bible is filled with norms birthed from behaviors and practices that result from a design.

A couple of examples would be God's instructions for building the Tabernacle. In this, we see God giving a blueprint or pattern for the building of the Tabernacle to Moses (Exodus 25-35). Notice the extreme detail and how God demanded the best to execute excellence. King Solomon was given a blueprint or design for the construction of the Temple (I Chronicles 28:11-19). Once again, give attention to God's demand for detail and excellence. Noah was given a pattern or blueprint for the building of the Ark (Genesis 6:7-22; 7:5). The Apostle Paul often used the language of a pattern (2 Timothy 1:13; 2:2). Learn these patterns, as from them many particle and useable protocols and etiquette may be formulated.

Notice that God established each of these patterns, which results in excellence. The study of God's usage of ways is an excellent start to selecting needed protocols and etiquette in the context of your ministry. There is no better foundation upon which to establish protocols and etiquette than that which derives from a biblical foundation. Whenever possible, the leader in the Kingdom of God will want to build protocols and etiquette on a "thus saith the Lord" or some principle established from the Word of God. While it is easy to take exception to a man's judgment, it is difficult to object to what is taken from God's Word.

Now let's put Bible patterns into action as we give an example of how one may use the Word of God to establish a protocol undergirded by etiquette. On any number of occasions, Christians in the early church would sing in their corporate assemblies (Ephesians 5:19; Colossians 3:16; Hebrews 2:12; James 5:19). As you read these and other scriptures, it becomes evident that the pattern was for the early Christians to sing songs and hymns in their assemblies. Singing then becomes a protocol.

To expedite the practice of singing today, the church may use a songbook to aid in carrying out the singing pattern; this would be considered etiquette. The singing is what the church does; that is "protocol." The use of the songbook as an aid to better carry out the practice of singing becomes the "etiquette." The point is that this all started with the pattern of singing seen in the Word of God and that employing the songbook as an etiquette is not unreasonable. The result is excellent, as the church does its best to give honor and glory to God.

Bible Principles

Etiquette

First, an appropriate place to start understanding how to develop protocols and etiquette based on Bible principles is to gain a definitional perspective of what is meant by "Biblical Principles." Allow me to point up two fundamental definitions of the use and application of the word "principle" as defined in Noah Webster's American Dictionary of the English Language: "A general sense, the cause, source or origin of anything; that from which a thing proceeds; as the principle of motion; the principles of action." Another definition of principle from this same resource reads: "A general truth; a law comprehending many subordinate truths; as the principles of morality, of law, of government, &c."(15) I intentionally selected this dictionary because it has an online resource which is based on the use of King James Version words, and extensively used in homeschooling and Bible study.

To be clear, a principle extracted from the Bible represents a general truth, a law comprehending many subordinate facts. This is our working definition of the "Bible Principle." Accordingly, when a student of the scriptures reads through the Bible, taking note of the number of general truths and the laws that teach subordinate truths provides the path to establishing any protocols supported by etiquette, all of which are based on the Word of God.

(15) Online Dictionary of King James Version words. Webster's 1828 Dictionary

The biblical principles may be ethical, moral, or spiritual, from the Old or New Covenants, the law, prophets, wisdom literature, gospels, history, and general or Pauline epistles. There are countless biblical resources from which to extract protocols and etiquette. It is simply the art of locating Bible principles and converting them into a protocol supported by any number of etiquettes that does not violate the Word of God.

Now let's sample this approach of using Bible principles to establish needed protocols and etiquette. The Bible teaches us to love one another (Mark 12:29). In hosting a guest for a church event, one may want to give gifts of love, such as a financial love offering. The event represents the protocol, the love offering reprints the etiquette. The Bible teaches that we should give honor to whom honor is due (Romans 13:7).

While encouraging dedicated members of your church, you may want to honor their works with a plaque or certificate of appreciation. The occasion would be the protocol, and the presentation of the plaque or certificate would be the etiquette. Suppose a minister or church leader was to counsel a sister in the congregation. In that case, a good practice may be to leave the office door open or have another sister present so that there is no perceived wrong or evil.

Does not the Bible teach us to avoid the very appearance of evil (I Thessalonians 5:22)? Does not the Bible teach us to present all things honestly in the sight of all men (2 Corinthians 8:21)? The idea of having the office door open sends the message there is honestly nothing going on wrong in the context of this private meeting between a brother and sister while counseling is taking place.

Counseling is the protocol, and the open door or additional person present is the etiquette. The point is that these protocols and etiquette have been designed and implemented based on Bible principles.

Bible Precepts

Etiquette

What is meant by "Bible Precept?" According to the International Standard Bible Encyclopedia, a precept is: "A commandment, an authoritative rule for action; in the scriptures generally, a divine injunction in which man's obligation is set forth." The word "commandment" in the New Testament, taken from the Greek word "entole," is used 68 times, but twice in the King James Version, it is translated as "precept" (Mark 10:5; Hebrews 9:19) (16).

The Bible is replete with commandments; while some are positive and others negative, they are all divine commands from God. There is much to learn from the Almighty as we survey His many orders that may be converted into practical protocols and etiquette. The commands of God represent how God deals with man. Using the same commands, we create protocols and etiquette, resulting in how men deal with one another.

(16) International Standard Bible Encyclopedia 1915

Now let's move on to sample using Bible precepts or commands to create protocols and etiquette. Allow me to point out a couple of Bible precepts or commands from the Old Testament and then draw down particle protocols and etiquette from these precepts.

Let's start with the Old Testament Bible. In the context of (Deuteronomy 4:2), Moses commanded the people of God not to add nor take away from the commandments given by God. In the Book of Wisdom, King Solomon wrote that the people of God were to know that every Word of God is pure and that they should trust Him. Therefore, they were instructed not to add unto His words (Proverbs 30:5-6). In these, we learn that God should be trusted; that becomes the protocol. Trust God. We must trust Him in every ministry, project, program, and spiritual effort. We trust Him when we have done all we know according to God's Word, way, and will, as revealed in His Holy Word. As an etiquette, the man of God may elect to hold prayer services, asking God to bless the works that have been set before Him; in this, a prayer service becomes an etiquette.

In the book of Daniel, Daniel offers a prayer on behalf of his people (Daniel 9:3-5). As Daniel prayed, he confessed sin because they had not kept the commandments of God. This was a moment of transparency and honesty on behalf of Daniel because of introspection. This disregard for the commandments of God teaches us the need for constant self-introspection. Respecting the commandments of God in every way becomes the protocol, and self-introspection becomes the etiquette.

These are but a sample to provide a framework of thinking as the church leader examines protocol needs and then supports the protocols with etiquette. In almost every facet of church ministry, something can be done to achieve excellence. This is how I have viewed establishing protocols; I make every effort to make them Bible-based. However, I realize that no one is smarter than God; there is very little about which God, either directly or indirectly, has not had something to say.

CHAPTER 3

A Minister for Every Ministry

Protocols

One of the highest callings in the land is preaching and teaching the gospel of our Lord Jesus Christ (2 Thessalonians 2:14; Romans 10:15). The God of salvation has clearly blessed so many with the gifts (Ephesians 4:7-8). Yet it is often difficult to determine the proper place to engage ministry.

Located ministry can often be confusing in the context of preaching and teaching for the right people in the right place. All churches are different; some are city churches, some are rural churches, some are numerically large, and others are numerically small. The education and socioeconomic and cultural dynamics are also different. How does a minister determine the best place for ministry?

When I was about to finish my undergraduate work in Memphis, Tennessee in the late 1980s, it seemed that every minister in the school wanted to minister to a large prestigious congregation, replete with a large building and ample leadership, staff, and members to get the work done. The question remained: Was this for me? Should I be looking for a smaller congregation that needs work to build those ministerial dream lists? Is it even necessary to have a large building, staff, and membership to consider oneself a part of a dynamic and effective ministry? The answer is that there is a ministry for every minister. Just as all churches are not alike, all ministers are not alike.

While for some this may be considered an uncomfortable topic of consideration, nevertheless it needs to be given great thought and examination. Therefore, let's examine several ministry scenarios, with the intent of getting a view of where a minister may best use talents and abilities to the glory of God and the upbuilding of His church.

Rural Church Ministry

Etiquettes

An article published in 2020 by Metro Voices News entitled "Rural Areas, Small Towns Still Have Almost Half Of All Churches," written by Alan Goforth, reports: "Nearly half of the country's congregations are in rural areas (25 percent) or small towns (22 percent), while the 2020 census found that only 6 percent of Americans live in rural areas and 8 percent in small towns."(11) This indicates the vast number of rural churches that need ministers to bring the Gospel of Jesus Christ and help rural churches survive. In addition, recent surveys indicate that nearly half of all churches in the southern states are in small towns and rural areas. Alan Goforth reports in this same article: "According to new data, half of the nation's congregations are in the South, even though only 38 percent of the U.S. population lives there. It also suggested that small congregations in rural areas and small towns may be unsustainable."

As churches in the rural areas of our nation become more culturally diverse, the door opens for a more diverse consideration as to whom it is that ministers in these rural area pulpits. In this same article, Goforth goes on to say:

"Congregations also are becoming more racially diverse. In 2000 only 12 percent of congregations were multiracial. In the latest survey, the figure climbed to 25 percent.

There is a bright spot in the movement of the nation's young people. The 2020 Census reveals that during Covid," (12)(11) (12) Rural areas and small towns still have almost half of all churches by Alan Goforth @ Widaman Communications, Inc. P.O. Box 1114; Lee's Summit, Mo. 64063

Yet the man of God has to entertain the consideration: Is rural ministry my calling? May I conduct ministry excellently while being spiritually, physically, mentally, and socially content in a rural church? The needed approaches to pastoral ministry are radically different from those of urban areas. Can a preacher function in a small or rural town where potential membership growth may be small in number and slow in results? Can you achieve excellence with practical ministries conducive to small-town needs? Will you be happy having to navigate a small-town mentality and cultural habits? If one has a family, would they be able to function in an area that may very well be limited with respect to shopping, entertainment, restaurants, and accessibility to essential medical resources? Are you the minister of this kind of ministry?

Over the years, I have encountered a number of ministers that prefer small-town, rural ministry. In some cases, these individuals have driven upwards of 100 or more miles one way to make their ministerial contributions to the Kingdom of God. The God we serve provides for every ministry need. The question before us is: Is this for you? Pray, ponder, and be practical as you analyze whether this is a good fit for you. It is better if you are sent by God than to attempt something that's not for you and discover that you just went and were not sent. Not every minister is built to handle the urban church experience, but this does not mean that God does not have a place for the preacher who does not favor the big city. There is a minister for this ministry.

Urban Church Ministry

Etiquettes

The urban church is composed of congregations located in many of the major inner cities and towns of our present world. When one thinks of the urban church, people tend to think of an inner city setting filled with the fast pace of downtown shopping, theater, and entertainment. Urban life is often inclusive of large homeless populations. In cities where gentrification has taken place, one will find a number of upper-middle-class families who may be career driven. The urban church calls for a minister who may be a commuter. This kind of ministry demands a minister that can deal with the fast pace of life.

The urban church ministry often calls for a more hands-on approach to meeting community needs; in addition to teaching and preaching, there may be a practical demand for works like food pantries, clothing closets, furniture depots, and drug and alcohol rehabilitation programs, all aimed to further the gospel of Jesus Christ. Street preaching has also been known to reach the inner-city masses effectively.

The question at hand is: Are you fit for the demands and needs of this kind of ministry? Not every minister could successfully carry the Gospel in an inner-city ministry. Taking on these custom-fit demands without personal introspection may result in a painful experience. Yet God has a man for every kind of ministry; again, the question remains: Is that you?

Over the years, I have witnessed several ministers who took on the first opportunity extended to them to preach without considering the demands that would await them as they propagated the gospel and engaged in ministry in an urban context. It is imperative that you take a close look at yourself as a minister, having evaluated your abilities, to determine if this is a dream or a nightmare about to happen. Just because you know the Bible and have excellent oratory skills may not, as a stand-alone, be enough to succeed in urban ministry.

If you are considering this type of assignment, speaking with someone with urban ministry experience may be a good idea. This will aid you in better evaluating whether you are the right minister for such a calling.

While there may be a few who do not think there is much need for inner-city ministers these days, I would point them to a survey article, "An Inside Look at Urban, Suburban, and Rural Communities and Churches," published by Christian Standard and written by Kent Fillinger, dated September 3, 2017. His research results yielded the following information: "The three-year average growth rate for downtown churches was the best of any location type (4.9 percent). The churches in older residential areas had the second-best growth rate (4.6 percent). By comparison, churches in older suburbs had the lowest average growth rate over the last three years (2.3 percent)." (13) This seems to imply that the need for inner-city ministers is in great demand, especially after considering recent population shifts and the success rate in urban church growth. But again, are you that minister?

(13) An Inside Look at Urban, Suburban, and Rural Communities and Churches, written by Kent Fillinger of the Christian Standard on September 3, 2017

Suburban Church Ministry

Etiquettes

In several cases, it is the suburban church ministry that comes to mind when most ministers think of building and contributing to the growth and stability of a local church. I well remember that while completing my undergraduate work in the early 1980s, most of the preachers about to graduate had a burning desire to go to the Bible Belt of the United States to preach in a state like Texas, which had large populations like Dallas, Houston, and Fort Worth. These were perceived as desirable suburban places with large memberships, significant buildings, and multi-site campus ministries.

The suburbs are filled with sleepy bedroom communities away from the hustle and bustle of the inner city and often filled with a population that seeks quiet, closeness, and community comforts like grocery stores, gas stations, and convenient shopping in almost every community.

Some have considered the suburban minister the coveted place and position to engage ministry. Not every minister is equipped to engage in suburban church ministry effectively. If you are uncomfortable being in a faster pace lifestyle, if you are intimidated dealing with a multicultural, diverse population filled with fast-track professionals, it is time to consider that suburban ministry may not be your calling.

It took me several years after becoming the Harlem Church of Christ minister in New York City, New York, to realize that I was in an environment completely different from my previous assignment in Pontiac, Michigan, a small town. This differed from the suburban ministry I enjoyed for 12 years in Memphis, Tennessee.

For the first time, I focused on the drastically different dynamics of geographical influences that impacted ministry right before my face. It is just a fact that a suburban church presents several demands a minister must evaluate. First, the man of God must understand that God loves all people (John 3:16). Resultantly, those in the suburbs who have fled the rat race of the inner cities have souls to be saved.

Now let's do some much-needed introspection. But first, can you handle the demands of preaching in a suburban setting?

The suburban minister has to have a sense of spiritual stamina and stability, as history and statistics stand to manifest a constant shift in populations in suburban living. This ministry is no place for a vulnerable ego. The most recent impact on suburban living has come about as a result of the Covid-19 global pandemic of 2020.

In an article published by Planetizen, "Suburban Revival: How 21st Century Will Redefine Life Outside the City," written by Chris Freda, Sara Egan, reported: "Following the suburbanization boom of the mid-20th century, it looked like Legacy Cities in places like the Northeast and the Rust Belt was in existential trouble. Planners, architects, developers, and urbanites alike were thrilled to see the reversal of this trend in the early 21st century as new segments of the population, including immigrants, Millennials, and empty nesters, began to rediscover inner cities.

For two decades now, Legacy Cities and boomtowns in the South, Southeast, and West have seen substantial growth and investment as cranes dotted skylines and ushered in a new era of urbanization. Throughout this time, suburban America struggled with population loss, aging infrastructure, and lifestyle offerings that seemed outdated and unresponsive to the needs of an increasingly cosmopolitan population. Ever swinging, the pendulums of economic pressures and societal preferences appear to be offering suburban places a second chance, as droves of people rediscover opportunity and community outside cities.

Suburbs in the largest metro areas throughout the country gained 4.7 million people since 2010. The population shift from urban areas to suburban communities has only been amplified by the COVID-19 pandemic, as more people prioritize privacy, increased living space, dedicated outdoor space, and other features that are increasingly difficult to access in dense urban environments.

The 2020 Census provides insight into this trend, reporting a record number of change-of-address requests to the United States Postal Service during the first six months of the pandemic. Attributes that planners have spent decades fighting to reverse—single-use land uses, low development densities, the proliferation of personal automobile travel, and a prioritization of private space—are again sought after by many who struggled through social isolation and physical confinement.

While the pandemic undoubtedly inspired broad swaths of the population to reconsider their priorities for living and working, growth in communities outside major cities is a trend with deeper roots. While many might prefer a more urban lifestyle—with its density, diversity, housing, transportation options, cultural vibrancy, and job opportunities—many cannot afford to live in big cities. Many of the same people who helped drive the early 20th-century re-urbanization trend are settling into careers, starting families, and exploring homeownership opportunities." (14)

This proves that the populations of our top American cities shift from time to time, which means the people of suburban churches move along these same lines. The question on the table is: Are you the minister for these kinds of dynamics?

Time nor room in these writings will permit me to point up an innumerable list of other ministry considerations such as the mission ministry, both domestic and foreign, the church planting ministry, college campus ministry, street ministry, and on the list goes. The notion here is for the minister to spend some much-needed time in examination, prayer, and practical introspection to determine in which direction he should look, and which is his calling, so when the time comes to engage ministry, he can give his best with excellence.

(14) Suburban Revival: How the 21st Century Will Redefine Life Outside the City.

By Chris Freda, Sara Egan November 7, 2021

CHAPTER 4

The Minister's First Church

Protocols

One of the most exciting times in a minister's life is the session where one is ready to look for the ministry's first work. Without a doubt, upon accepting the call to the church, the overwhelming excitement about getting started is ever-present.

But how does a minister go about finding the first local church work? How does such a minister engage in the interview process? Moreover, how does he determine if this is the right fit for him?

These are among the questions to be covered in this chapter. After training over 18 preachers and having served three churches in three distinctly different parts of the United States, these are a few tested and tried considerations that may help as you look for your first assignment.

There is a statement made with your first church assignment. You can set your focus and create a clear path to progress and success by the relative choice you make on vetting and accepting your first ministry assignment. A wise and prudent man will carefully consider the cost and not enter blindly into such an important springboard as this.

The Minister's First Church Search

Etiquettes

As a preacher starts to search for the first work assignment, he will want as much as humanly possible to gravitate away from historically troubled churches. These churches have become widely known for experiencing severe complications in enjoying longevity in a preacher, leadership, or congregation relationship.

As sad as it may be, many churches make it a practice of changing preachers every few years. It is unfair for a preacher to be expected to move his entire life from one location to another to see if it will all work out. What's more, it is not fair to a local congregation for them to adjust to a new preacher to have the relationship severed in a short period; it is an unacceptable experience for both parties. This search session requires a preacher's insightfulness, honesty, and sober mindedness. Beware of taking a blind leap into unfamiliar territory, having done no due diligence.

No minister of the Gospel of Jesus Christ should be content with being a part of what some call "the dog and pony show." The dog and pony show is when a church ministerial search committee requests that so-called candidates apply, replete with three personal references, clearing a background and credit check, the submission of a recent sermon recorded on a DVD, and a visit to the local church to preach on Sunday morning and Sunday night and teach two Bible classes on Sunday and Wednesday respectively. Will someone please help the world understand what this is designed to accomplish for the good of the local church, let alone the preacher himself?

If a preacher does not have two great sermons, two great Bible class messages, and good friends willing to recommend him, he should not be in ministry. If by chance a minister currently holds any position at all in another local congregation, such as an assistant minister, youth minister, someplace in church administration, or the like, and the church where you currently labor finds out you are searching for work, often because the word has gotten back home before you even return. They may determine to help you out the door before you have been offered any ministerial opportunity.

This is an unfair and unwise approach to receiving a new preacher ministry. In the judgment of many, a local church should look over the world and select a first and second choice that is in the best interest of the local work. Then offer the work to the first choice; if he accepts the offer to bring his ministry to that local congregation, the list is complete.

If the first choice says God is leading him in another direction, then and only then should the church move on and offer the opportunity to the second choice. This removes the dog and pony or gospel competition circus approach.

Beware Of Hiring Hooks

Etiquettes

In several instances, a ministerial search group will comprise of leadership want-to-be's. These men suggest that they would like to recommend you as the new preacher to the congregation and welcome you to bring your ministry to the community but will only do so based on certain binding conditions.

Conditions like, "You must be willing to ordain us as elders or leaders if you want to work with this congregation." Others may advance the notion that you will have a short window to identify, train and ordain them as leaders if you want the work. Not only is this unspiritual, unethical, and immoral, it is equally impractical. After all, chances are you do not know these men and would have no idea if they meet the scriptural character pictures recorded in (I Timothy 3:1-7; Titus 1:5-9).

Other proposed conditions may sound like this: "If you become the new minister here, you must unquestionably submit to our rule. We are in total control; you are our employee and must agree to be subservient to our authority."

This is also an unscriptural, unethical, and immoral request. Nowhere in scripture does God command ministers to be employees and be blindly subservient to anyone other than God Himself. This is a concept that God heard about from men, not that which men heard about from God, and recorded on the pages of inspiration.

In the life of ministers, there is any number of unmarried persons; this means they are single. Yet some churches insist that as a condition of consideration for the church to be willing to receive a preacher's ministry, the preacher will be given a short, identified window of time to find and marry a spouse. This is also another unreasonable proposed condition. There is no indication anywhere in the Holy Scriptures that marriage must be a condition of serving a local congregation as her minister. The Apostle Paul never had a wife and seemingly had the gift of celibacy (I Corinthians 7:7).

There is always the one-year hook. The one-year angle advances the notion that we will give this a trial run for one year and then evaluate the preacher's performance and fit for the congregation. At this time, one may be terminated without a stated cause. In most cases, this trial run has no promises of a future.

Let it be said in another way: "If we do not like you after the first year, we will expect you to move on." Who would be willing to uproot their lives and move across the state or nation, perhaps even leave an excellent secular job, all for a trial run?

This reeks of instability and uncertainty about the decision to receive one's ministry. This must be viewed as a preverbal flag that should not be ignored.

The Interview Process

Etiquettes

For ministers whose interest in a local congregation has been taken seriously and appears to have done well in the early exchange between a search committee and a minister, the next probable step is "the interview process." In the pre-pandemic period of our culture, this process would more often than not be held in person. While in these post-pandemic times, it is not at all uncommon for the interview process, or initial interview process, to be conducted via Zoom, FaceTime, or some other popular multi-media approach.

As a rule, the interview process is led by a search committee, replete with sometimes a number of doctrinal and practical questions designed to familiarize the committee with the minister, his views on scripture, his level of communication skills, and his level of perceived abilities. All said and done, the interview process has been designed for the committee to see what a minister has to offer, both his strengths and weaknesses.

Allow me to quickly point out the fact that the interview process is a two-way street. In other words, while the committee interviews a minister, at the same time, the minister should be interviewing the search committee or at least be pointed to those who may best answer his questions. This is not just about the life of the church; it is also about the life of the minister as well.

Let me point out a few considerations that should be at the forefront of a minister's mind as he interviews the local church. It is not unreasonable to question their expectations of one who serves as their minister. How many active members are there in the role of the church, what is the church's annual projected financial budget, and how often does the church actually meet that projected budget? How deep in debt is the congregation in terms of annual financial obligations, annual reoccurring notes, mortgages, and the like? It is all too common for a church to be in deep debt and never mention it to a minister interviewing for the work, until after the arrival takes place.

Ministers need a clear transparent understanding about the governance of that local congregation, who and how spiritual determinations are made. It should be admitted that it is not a bad idea to have a few questions about how the church's by-laws are read. Much of what is not stated in an interview process concerning the governance of the local church has been clearly stated in the by-laws of that local church, sometimes without the knowledge of the congregation at large. Who are the officers of the church's legal structure? Is there a proposed contract to be read and negotiated between the two representatives at the interview table?

What is the congregation's view of the role, scope, and function of a minister? Is there room for growth in financial support from the congregation, and on what basis? The interview process cannot be permitted to be one-sided.

This is a perfect time for the interested minister to voice clear expectations of the leadership and local congregation. Someone once said, "Good understanding in the front makes for no misunderstandings in the rear."

The Contract Consideration

Etiquettes

In the eyes of a growing number of preachers, the notion of a contract has become a target of scrutiny. Not merely in terms of the presence of a contract, as much as the content of the contract. A contract is worth no more than the integrity of the signatories. There are far too many cases where church leaders have signed a contract with little or no intentions of keeping all the terms of that contract. The last thing a minister wants is the reputation of having taken the Lord's church to court over a contractual dispute.

At the same time, a contract may be a good thing in order to accomplish clarity, especially for those who were not at the table at the time the contract was negotiated and agreed upon. The contract may also remove any ambiguity about the expectations of both parties-- minister and congregation. The contract may best be structured and worded so as to not appear to be a payment for services rendered agreement. Is it really possible to pay a minister for every aspect and consideration associated with the work of ministry?

The biblical model of ministerial compensation looks more like full maintenance, while the minister moves about to engage ministry locally, regionally, nationally, and worldwide (I Corinthians 9:3-12). Again, this is not a payment for services rendered agreement. The local congregation does have the authority to determine if they should provide financial support to the minister, just how much.

If a contract is in play, it may be best to include details such as the length of the contract, expected financial compensation amounts, the days on which it is to be expected, clarity about vacation time, intervals of increases in financial compensation, and by how much if determinable, a list of benefits, whether the minister is W-2 or 1099, who is responsible for paying social security taxes, the expectations regarding office hours, off days, sick pay just to name a few contractual considerations.

If God is good, a minister will not have the kind of challenges that cannot be resolved internally. In the event that they are troubles that cannot be settled equitably, it may be a fair consideration to have an arbitration clause inserted into a minister's contract.

In the arbitration consideration, one would be wise to recommend that no less than 3-4 nationally noted ministers be invited in to hear and settle the crisis at hand. The arbitrator's final recommendations should be considered as binding, meaning all parties would be willing to abide by their counsel.

This is not designed to provide a Christian polemic against nor in favor of the presence of a contract. These are thought-provoking observations that should come to mind in view of a contractual consideration.

The possibility of ministerial termination and subsequent parting of the ways is never a pleasant experience. In this regard, some consideration to separation compensation should be considered while negotiating the contract.

No minister should ever consider accepting the spiritual blessings and burdens of local ministry solely based on a moral majority consensus of a minister search committee or a moral majority consensus of a leadership that was sealed by the signing of a contract.

So often, this is done separately and apart from the more than moral majority consensus of the local congregation. The principle of moral majority consensus of the local church may be clearly seen in the context of (Acts 6:5-6). This is offered as a principle and not the law of this context.

Should a minister work within the context of local church ministry without a contract? While this is certainly doable, it may not be advisable, while all circumstances are different, this may relegate to a matter of wisdom.

Do Your Due Diligence

Etiquettes

The consideration of taking on a first work requires a tremendous amount of prayer and research. This is a time when one may want to have a much-needed transparent conversation with the previous minister. This must be an open-eyed conversation, as you endeavor to be perceptive enough to determine if the past minister is bitter or angry over the experience of separating from the work he has recently parted from. A few questions about that person's experience with the church and her leadership and the reason or reasons for the departure from the work could be insightful and, in fact helpful, especially if the congregation has had a high turnover of ministers in rapid succession. In addition, a small bit of background research with other ministers and churches in the area, those who may know a little about the history of the congregation, cannot hurt. In fact, it may prove to be beneficial.

There are few churches in the world today that do not have some sort of identifiable track record. Often that track record will reveal the longevity or lack thereof concerning her minister's tenure. Even among those outside the Body of Christ. The notion here is to do your research. To be foretold is to be forewarned.

Do not get caught up in the flattery and amusement of a church having interest in you to the end that you do not do some standard investigation into the church's track record. I have often thought it shameful the number of congregations who, with little regard for men and their families, do short-term trial runs with ministers and end up going through ministers like a change of daily clothing.

Due diligence also carries with it the idea of looking into the more influential people involved in the interview process. Give special attention to the person in the room that seems to have the ability to sway others to their positions, almost like having a bully in the room. It is not uncommon for that person to be in control of the church's checkbook or in control of the congregation's finances. There is something about men and the madness of money. In some people's minds control of the money equals control of the major decisions concerning selecting a new minister.

It is also a good idea to talk with ministers who have frequented the congregation as a guest minister in revivals, gospel meetings, workshops, and the like over recent years. Such a person may have a good feel for the workings of a local congregation and, to a great extent, have a clearer view of what you are about to get yourself into.

It may be a sad commentary, yet there are an untold number of churches that are in bad financial conditions. They never let on that you are being interviewed for a church whose doors are on the verge of closing because of their inability to pay down their debts.

Let's now turn our attention to a few inner family considerations. Should one be a married person, be perceptive concerning your family's feelings about the work for which you are being considered? Some wise person said, "Happy wife, Happy life." After all, your family is an important part of the whole due diligence equation.

Perhaps one of the most insightful things that may be done by a minister looking into his first work is reading the members of the local congregation themselves. While you may be well received by a pulpit search committee, the question remains, how are you being received by the people you will be serving? You do not want to ignore the moral majority consensus of the church membership.

Do everything you can within reason to understand, read and know what you are really considering as you look at your first work or any work for that matter.

CHAPTER 5

First-Year Fundamentals

Protocols

The first years in a new ministry are one of the most critical times of a minister's tenure in a new work. If ministerial histories have proven nothing, they have proven the fact that the preacher who does the most effective work on a local church level are those who enjoy long tenure. In other words, you ought to be planning to stay as opposed to moving around every few years to a new work. Constant moving is not good for the local church, nor is it good for you and your family, should you have one.

In your first or early years, especially your first year, your mission is to establish yourself as an authority in the scriptures, one who is obviously studious and an ever learning and growing minister. The church needs to see and know that you are knowledgeable of the scriptures. A sound church is built on the Word of God, not singing, programs, or congregational ministries as a standalone, but the Word of God.

At all costs, never engage in the practice of immediately attempting to make corrections and changes in the structure, organization, administration, and ministries of the congregation. As hard as it may be, do not attempt to change the principal finance person, or the church secretary, or the church administrator, or men who have previously been in leadership. During that first year, just watch, take written and mental notes, and notice what is working and what has not been working, but do not make any changes until you know where the pitfalls are and who you are up against when attempting to make changes.

This session requires wisdom and patience as you prepare yourself and the people for any needed changes. Most people and churches do not deal with changes well. It really is a slow and methodical process. In most cases, you will have a two-year window to change the homeostasis of a given church. The change in congregational paradigms in most churches is a really slow process. If you move too fast, you may tear up more than you will find yourself building up. Take this time to learn the membership, the real disciples, the difficult personalities, the discouraged saints, the preacher pushers, and the preacher haters.

How to Halt a Honeymoon

Etiquettes

For most ministers, the early years are considered "the honeymoon." You are new to the church, they are new to you, and everyone, for the most part, seems excited about future growth and development under a new minister. One of the quickest ways to prematurely terminate a honeymoon is what I like to call "The Spend Down." The "Spend Down" goes like this: every time you make a change most leadership will want to go along with it even if they do not necessarily agree with it. They want you and the church to do well together, so they buy into it. But you have started the process of spending favors.

The next time you recommend what you feel is a needed change, leadership again won't kick against the recommendation, even though they do not like it, or for that matter, agree with the proposed change. Before you know it, at the very next proposed change, the feel and tone of relationships between you and leadership starts to feel different. Passive aggressiveness (those not publicly against you but won't do anything to help you) on the part of the leadership and sometimes even the membership becomes the new tone.

The problem is that you started making far too many changes way too early in your ministry, and every time you do that, you spend a favor until you have used up all the favors you have coming, and the honeymoon is now over. Do not attempt to make these changes too early on in your ministry; you may bring an early halt to your honeymoon. Over the years, I have seen this happen to a number of preachers who did too much too early, and it worked against them and not for them.

Ease your way into what you have identified as needed changes. If sin and destruction of the church are not at play, wait it out--it will work to your advantage. Often patience is not a virtue of youth, and with a number of younger ministers, the propensity is to move too fast. Preacher, you must learn to spend your favors wisely and not wistfully.

Lay Hands on No Man Suddenly

Etiquettes

This is the perfect time to remember that you are new to this church and do not know who is who. It is not uncommon for some brother to attempt to befriend the new minister. What you did not know is that all the time this brother had bad motives. There is a principle found in the context of (I Timothy 5:22), that may serve the man of God well. There the Apostle Paul advised young Timothy, "Lay hands suddenly on no man."

It takes time to learn people to discern the well-intended from the not so well intended. Often some have a hidden agenda to which you do not want to fall victim. Is this brother someone who has leadership aspirations, knowing all the while that he could never meet the character qualities of (I Timothy 3 and Titus 1)? The possibilities are endless as to the impure motives of the masses.

Be cautious about that person who wants to help purchase you a new car or personally help you with the down payment on a place to live. Minister, just be careful that these situations do not come back to haunt you. Learn to be friendly and approachable, yet not so common with people that you have not been around long enough to really know that you leave yourself vulnerable. Preacher, lay hands on no man suddenly!

Never allow yourself to become overly familiar with the brothers, do not drop your guard and engage in tasteless jesting, comments about the sisters, trying to be accepted as just another one of the guys. Being too familiar will cause you to crash.

Men's Money and Madness

Etiquettes

It has never ceased to amaze me what money can do to good men. I still cannot understand why the notion of being in control of the church's checkbook makes some men feel they are in complete control. The Book is correct (I Timothy 6:10). There the Bible reads: "For the love of money is the root of all evil...." Nonetheless, some feel they will have control over your life and ministry because they are the signatories of your paycheck.

Quickly learning where the power struggles lie is always a good idea. Early on in your ministry is not a good session to go to war with the powers that be, especially the man that holds the church's checkbook. You are up for a battle of the worst proportion. If you are a faithful Bible teacher, the teaching of the Word of God will float him to the top, and soon all will be able to see his ill motives and that such a person is not Kingdom driven.

Do not be surprised if such a person is far more corporate than he or she is Kingdom. There is still a number among the people of God who think because they have been successful in the world that it somehow makes them experts in a Kingdom spiritual agenda. It is all just madness, yet God will provide.

The poison of power plays often prove to be a pitfall that may lead to the termination of the new preacher's preverbal honeymoon. This is when there are people who have been in positions of influence before your arrival and feel obligated to guard and protect their perceived position of influence. As pointed out in the previous chapter, by all means, never move too fast to dethrone or remove influential people (people who have a strong following within the congregation) from their coveted positions. Oftentimes, these are people with congregational tenure or people who know just a little more scripture than the masses.

Sometimes they are intellectual bullies who hold academic degrees in other fields of study besides theology but have convinced themselves that they are more informed because they are more educated than others. This can prove to be a trap when the decision is made to take them on to the end of removing them. The results tandem out to a session of conflict and sheer madness. At the end of the day, your session of comfort, open communication, and non-conflict will result in the early termination of your new honeymoon with the church.

Plan Your Work and Work Your Plan

Etiquettes

The value of one's session of observation will pay off once you transition to the next stage in the early years of a new work. That next stage comes after you have carefully observed and planned needed constructive modifications and changes to the church's present structure. Now you are ready for the implementation process. This is also a time when having established yourself as a student of scripture during your first years will provide you with an opportunity to recommend your needed changes based on Bible principles. This puts people in the position to have to argue with the Bible and not with the minister.

It is time to employ biblical principles of delegation, which are replete throughout the Bible. Moses used delegation in order to make constructive changes to better serve the people of God (Exodus 18:24-27). In the context of (Acts 6:2-6), the apostles used delegation to bring greater order to the problem of neglect concerning the Grecians who complained about being overlooked in the daily ministration.

With respect to building and strengthening of the local church, that is engaging the missions of local church growth.

There are four considerations that come to mind. First, the local church needs a balanced and relevant pulpit. The pulpit is not a place for ministerial hobby riding. Aim to provide the church with a balanced healthy diet of preaching and teaching that is designed to be relevant. Second, develop or select a dynamic Bible teaching curriculum that is age appropriate and frame it as a school that teaches the Bible. Third, every church needs an evangelistic movement.

The difference between an evangelism program or ministry and an evangelistic movement is realized in the church buying into the need to spread the Gospel to the masses and make disciples of men (Matthew 28:19-20). Once new converts are indoctrinated with the need to share the gospel with others and then start inviting other family and friends to be taught the gospel, a kind of evangelism fire gets started. This is how churches grow as opposed to swelling by way of those who are already Christians placing membership. The placing of membership simply moves members around from one place to another. This is not church growth; this is church swelling. Plan your work and then work your plan.

CHAPTER 6

Changing of the Guard

Protocol

"The changing of the guard" is a traditional reference to the idea of a minister stepping down and a new minister taking up the works of a local church. There are a number of considerations that need to be given time and concern in order for this process to be healthy for both the minister and the church, respectively. In many cases, the previous minister may plan to remain as what some congregations call a "Minister Emeritus," or moving forward he may serve the church as one of her elders or as some other part of the church's leadership team. It goes without saying that this could be a challenging scenario.

What are the right and wrong things to do when the previous minister stays around? How does a new minister deal with the church when the last minister elects to remain after one has relinquished all ministerial duties and there needs to be a changing of the guard? For that matter, how does the new minister deal with the previous minister without disrespecting him?

Transparency Transition and Transference Etiquettes

There are three considerations that need to be talked about and then executed in the context of a changing of the guard. It is not at all uncommon for a lot of misunderstandings to take place because there have been no transparent conversations about the needed components of this entire process, and it is a process. Transition will always occur long before actual transference happens. It takes an undefined period of time for a person to unravel years, if not decades, of life and ministry before being able to move on.

The notion of transition has to do with the previous minister identifying all of the personal considerations at play that will allow him to move to the transference. Often this has to do with settling all residual financial obligations of the church with the minister and those that the minister has with the church. This may include things like a house purchased, leased, or rented in the church's name, a car leased or purchased in the church's name, any considerations relative to separation pay, equipment currently in the possession of the previous minister that is rightly owned by the church and the list goes on.

Coming to an agreement that is acceptable to all parties concerned is a part of this transition process. All parties need to be open and transparent about which matters should be considered within the context of this process. This is done earnestly to avoid misunderstandings or appearing to be non-cooperative with the transition process.

What, if any, financial obligations will the church have to the previous minister after the transition period has ended? This has often been proven to blindside the incoming minister simply because it was not discussed transparently. Some wise man once said, "Good understanding in the front makes for no misunderstanding in the rear."

The actual transference of all ministerial responsibilities previously enjoyed by the outgoing minister is the final leg of this changing of the guard process. Given that as many conceivable situations as possible have been visited, it is now time for the previous minister to relinquish his charge and duties to the church. The point here is that this really is a process. How long the process of transition and transference may take is also a matter of concise discussion.

The Previous Minister Is Still Here

Etiquettes

In a number of instances, the previous minister remains as some part of the church's spiritual life moving forward. One of the most detrimental things a minister new to a church can do is publicly or otherwise appear to disrespect the previous minister. The church is often filled with people that the previous minister has converted, taught, counseled, married, and mentored. The last thing a new minister wants to do is to engorge that minister's influences. A smart practice is, from time to time, simply acknowledge the previous minister's presence and openly project the fact that there is a healthy relationship between the two of you. On occasions when the new minister plans to be away on preaching assignments, invite the previous minister to preach in your absence. When expedient, go to him for counsel and guidance even if you do not take his advice, it speaks volumes that you respected him enough to even inquire.

On the other hand, the previous minister has to have the wisdom to know when and where to move out of the way of the new minister's leadership. He also has a part to play in helping the church move forward and execute in a way that does not hinder the work. In cases where the present leadership rejects the notion of the previous minister's involvement, becomes the perfect time to remind them of his ongoing influences with the current membership.

Carefulness needs to be exercised—do not be guilty of taking part in the poor prejudiced judgments of others. This may hurt you, not help you. The fact that the church is able to discern that there is an equitable relationship between the both of you will always work to your advantage. In this regard, you are building your own influence with the church by your godly example.

Much of what works and does not work will relegate to the persons and personalities involved. Sadly, there are far too many cases when a previous minister has been forced out of ministry against his will; resultantly, he may be bitter and not cooperative with needed processes. In such cases, you must opt to guard your own spiritual integrity, and stay the course in regard to what you know is the right thing to do.

After all, at the end of the day, this is about the health of the church and not just the ministers involved. Much prayer, patience, and common-sense protocols will become your salvation. If your presence in this new work is, in fact, the will of God, be sure He will have the final word and protect the spiritual integrity of your mission. The changing of the guard is a sensitive, vulnerable, and critical step in the church moving forward seamlessly.

A Big Head Will Only Burst

Etiquettes

There is absolutely no place in ministry for a big ego. Big egos and ministry do not make for a growing healthy culture in the context of the church. Humility should become the order of the day. If you make the mistake of placing too much confidence in your personal abilities, knowledge, and experience with your ministry assignment, be sure that a big head will only burst.

No one likes the look or feel of someone who presents as though they know it all. Being resistant to the ideas and input of other experienced Kingdom workers will only garner a hostile working environment. It never hurts anyone to hear the visions of others, even in times when you strongly feel that the visions and input are misguided. There are those who have already traveled the road you are now on. They have had the experience of scraping their knees on the preverbal sidewalks of church work. Listen and learn from the fruits of their journey, and benefit from what could be counsel. Avoid at all costs the big head syndrome.

This is a great session to reach out to others who have been through what you are presently experiencing. Factor in the warnings, exhortations, and advice that may come from the paths they have already traveled. Do not ever convince yourself that no one understands the challenges of being in a new church ministry other than yourself. This is the devil's trap; you are probably setting yourself up for failure. To be foretold is to be forewarned.

Every church is different; what works in one church may quickly fail in your current ministry. Do not abstain from the idea that others have figured out a few things you have not. A big ego may wrongly influence you to turn a deaf ear to guidance sent to you by the Almighty Himself.

Big Shoes, But I Have Little Feet

Etiquettes

As time moves on there are a growing number of tenured ministers who are either retiring from located ministry or have been called home by the Lord from labor to reward. A goodly number of these soldiers of the cross have enjoyed larger-than-life legacies during their years of service in the Kingdom.

A select few of these servants have been gospel trailblazers, taking the gospel where others have not, establishing dynamic trends in converting disciples, building large congregations, and building admirable facilities to the glory of God and the upbuilding of the Kingdom. When it is all said and done, these are they to whom reference is being made, when it is said they appear to have "big shoes" to fill.

The "little feet" portion of this ministry etiquette refers to a group of good and godly ministers that do not come to the table with that already established "larger than life" metaphorical shoes. Often, this is in fact their first ministry with a local congregation. It goes without saying that this particular set of circumstances can be intimidating.

How in the world does a minister come behind a gospel giant in the faith, a great church builder, and an international preacher of the cross of Calvary? He may feel like he is faced with the task of filling "big shoes with little feet."

Preacher, every minister of the gospel of Jesus Christ is different. Your God assignment may be different, your reason for being a part of this church may be different, and what the Lord expects you to accomplish may be different. Your mission has absolutely nothing to do with attempting to fill the shoes of the minister that preceded you. Establish your own shoes of contribution to the work. If you invest your time and energy in trying to be someone else, if you try to live up to someone else's standards, you rob yourself and the church of the unique contributions that God sent you to make.

More importantly, people may easily be able to see what you are not contributing to, but competing with the works that have gone on before your arrival, never attempt to be anyone other than yourself. There is only one you on the earth, and no one can beat you being you. On one occasion, the Apostle Paul pointed out the fact that it is "God that gives the increase" (I Corinthians 3:6).

This should not be your focus; you are not a part of this church to prove you can do as much or more than the previous minister. You are on a God assignment, and God will provide you with your own shoes, to His honor and glory, according to His own purpose over your life and ministry.

This framework of thinking constitutes a tremendous pitfall and drawback to the otherwise good that may be accomplished in the context of your works in the church.

It should be acknowledged that all of us have some shadow of influence in us, from our teachers, mentors, and fathers in the gospel, and for that matter, a preacher who preceded you. Yet you do not want to preach like, sound like, dress like, or have the identical influences like someone else because of their perceived successes. Forget about the shoes; just enjoy your own walk and work. This is an excellent consideration for anyone who is new to a position or appointment--never try to compete with the example of your predecessor. Just be yourself.

Traditional Leadership Legacies

Etiquettes

In a number of churches across the world today may be found those who are proud of the leadership models that they believe have worked for them down through the years. These leadership models range from the biblically organized churches (Philippians 1:1), to those who have enjoyed any number of traditional structures, such as a

Board of Trustees, a Board of Deacons, a Leadership Quorum (seven men), Leading Brothers, Concerned Brethren, Leadership Committee, Majority Rule Church Meetings, and the like.

With the changing of the guard (meaning there is now a new minister in the equation), the notion of how leadership operates is not an uncommon point of concern. In the majority of cases, there is some form of leadership already intact upon the arrival of a new minister. This is also a traditional time for those who previously were rejected as potential leaders to rise up and demand fresh consideration.

The Pressures of a Passive-Aggressive Leadership

One of the most difficult and uncomfortable matters for a new minister is the passive aggression often displayed among some in leadership. Passive aggression simply means that there are those who will not directly address the minister's preaching, programs, or ministry projections, nor will they openly oppose him. But they will indirectly sabotage many of the work-driven efforts advanced by the new minister. More often than not, those who practice passive aggression may not oppose you publicly or openly but will be sure to do nothing whatsoever to help advance that which is against their personal views or agendas. Sometimes they won't openly attempt to hurt the minister; they just do everything conceivable to not help. It often feels like someone smiling in your face, but as soon as you turn around, they stab you in your back.

Now, you have been placed in the position of attempting to avoid confrontation with your leaders at all costs. It is only fair to point out the fact that this can be quite stressful and transpose into pressure. Be ready for the fight of your life if you even remotely suggest that the leadership model needs to be changed. You may even need to have a U-Haul truck reserved because your next step may be out the door.

But how do you know that you may be dealing with a passive-aggressive leadership? When you walk into a room where your leaders are gathered, and a conversation suddenly stops, and you encounter a dry welcome, but no indication is made known about the content of the previously held conversation, most likely you are encountering passive aggression from your leaders. Have you ever been in a meeting with the church to present a new program, project, or ministry, and while the presentation is going on, your leaders are looking down at the floor, or they offer no visible support to your presentation? Most likely you are feeling the reactions of passive-aggressive leaders.

The most effective way to deal with a passive-aggressive leadership is with the Word of God. Your salvation rests in the scriptures. The Word of God will always float dysfunctional behavior to the top. If the matter feels like one of a personal nature, a study is needed of (Matthew 18:15-17). If you stay with the scriptures, the argument is not with you personally but with the Word of God. In instances where your leaders are murmuring to others about their displeasures concerning your ministry, a study may be needed of texts like (Philippians 2:14-16).

As a rule, passive-aggressive leaderships do not engage you directly; they work around you, which may result in division. These are those who need a study of (I Corinthians 1:10). The absolute wrong way to deal with passive aggression is to be drawn into conflict. Preacher, never allow yourself to be drawn into the appearance of striving with passive-aggressive leaders. Remember the Apostle Paul's exhortation to young Timothy (2 Timothy 2:24-26). Remain spiritual, and your response to these kinds of pressures should always be with the Word of God.

CHAPTER 7

The Winds of Change

Protocols

There is any number of changes to be expected, and in fact anticipated, during a minister's years of labor in the context of local church work. A minister's very reason for being a part of a church is to effect change for the good and growth of that church. This innately means there will be change. Yet change can be tricky, especially if it is unwanted change. What could be worse is if the change cuts against the grain of spiritual and numerical growth within the congregation.

I well remember a number of years ago, as I went to take my customary seat in the pulpit stage area, I was seated next to the minister emeritus, Dr. R. C. Wells. After about a half hour Dr. Wells blurted out, "The winds of change are blowing." After services ended, I asked him what he meant by "the winds of change are blowing." He made the observation that he noticed an obvious drop in attendance at the corporate assembly; a number of otherwise faithful attendees were now absent. At the time, we had overflow crowds; we were converting and baptizing over 100 people every year. If you did not get to services early, chances were you could not find a place to sit.

Not long after, it came to our attention that one of the church's trustees was starting rumors that the leadership was not making wise decisions about the spending of the church's monies. He contended that Dr. Wells and I had too much influence over the membership. Families started to leave and attend other churches. A number of members stopped attending the corporate assembly (at least until the controversy was settled). Others came but had a dry-damped spirit.

In this context, the winds of change were starting to blow. I was determined to confront the trustee about his allegations. In turn, an investigation committee was appointed of eight men to examine all the minutes from past leadership meetings, a review of all bank records was conducted, and the determination was made that there were no misappropriations of any kind found. The investigative committee held a public meeting with the church and revealed their findings.

Within two weeks, attendance started to return to normal, and the spirit of the congregation started to feel healthy again. The winds of change were once again blowing, but this time in a spiritually healthy direction. It was at this time that I learned a valuable lesson. Sometimes, members will stop attending the corporate assembly, not because they are for or against any one position, but because they do not come to the public assembly to deal with negativity.

Preacher, make every effort not to take it personally when people decide to stay away from perceived church problems. It is not an indictment against you personally; people really do not like church controversy.

Preacher Winds

Etiquettes

When a preacher is new to a church, it is an excellent time to remember that the membership and leadership do not know you. They have never worked with you, nor do they know your strengths and weakness as a Kingdom worker. This in itself is enough to cause potential instability. On the other side of this matter is the fact that the new preacher also does not know the memberships and leadership strengths and weaknesses. This can be a volatile session for all parties involved.

As the membership, leadership, and new preacher start the process of getting to know one another, it is not uncommon for a spirit of apprehension to set in. As a rule, the feeling of excitement will meet you upon your arrival. But do not be alarmed if the "let's wait and see where all of this is going" mindset is at the forefront. In this regard, the winds of change may start to blow. There are a number of things about which a new preacher should not be overly concerned.

Patience is the order of the day. It takes time for all parties to get to know each other. Some members may even stop attending services, while others may deal with you with a hands-off kind of feel.

Here, Preacher, is one of a number of situations when you can anticipate that the winds of change will blow. Do your work and resist the inclination to take things so personally. In due time it will become evident if there is a real ministerial marriage between the Master (Jesus Christ), the man (Preacher), and the membership (Church Body), inclusive of her leadership. Things are not as bad as they may feel; this is just an innate part of the ministry bonding process.

In 2000, I was appointed the new minister to a congregation where the previous minister had served for over 50 years. Upon my arrival, there was a feeling of excitement in the air every Sunday and mid-week. It wasn't long before I started feeling what I thought was an "us against him" kind of spirit. I became alarmed because I saw that the winds of change were blowing. Instead of reacting, I determined to give it more time, and it was then that I saw that things started relaxing. After some real introspection, I had to remind myself that the membership did not know me, at least not as their minister. It forced me to consider the fact that change was viewed by some as unsettling and foreign. It was not an indictment against me or my leadership, it was as simple as unfamiliarity.

In this regard, let's talk about the change in congregational homeostasis. I can think of nothing more important to the church's growth and development than stability. When changes take place in the church, members often feel unstable. The instability results from having to depart from that with which they had been comfortable or that they had come to feel was normal. Be patient and watch the winds start to blow in a more stable direction. Time and transition go hand in hand.

Leadership Winds

Etiquettes

There is no church in the world that has not been accused of operating in a way that is most comfortable for them. Without introducing a theological debate regarding biblical and traditional leadership models, the fact remains that the congregation would not permit nor follow if they were not in some way comfortable. You are the new kid on the block, if you will. You are the new face in this equation. As is the case with the membership, and so is the case with the church's leadership; the two of you aren't accustomed to working together.

One of the things that may cause the winds of change to blow in the arena of church leadership is when a new minister starts leaning in the direction of recommending that the faces in the current leadership need to change. This is a dangerous and unwise pursuit. Often people can become territorial and offended when their leadership is questioned. The response may sometimes sound like this: "I have been with this church through thick and thin. I am by far the most tenured member of this leadership team," or "I have more influence in this church than this new preacher. The church will follow me." This mindset manifested by these leaders speaks volumes. It tells you that real troubles may be brewing.

When confronting a situation where toxic leadership is a problem, your only salvation is the Word of God. Sound and careful teachings taken from the Bible concerning biblical leadership tend to float bad leadership selections to the surface.

In this instance, the argument is with the Bible and not with the preacher. While it is not uncommon to receive pushback at the mere thought of teaching on leadership, this is not enough to remove the God component of the Holy Scripture. Preachers, there is nothing like a "thus saith the Lord" moment. Wisdom may necessitate the start of a leadership training class.

Make it a point to do the training in the ear, sand, and eyes of the membership, so that everyone is clear about the teachings of the Bible concerning scriptural leadership. After all, your job is to "set in order the things that are wanting and ordain elders in every city" (Titus 1: 5). Yet do not make the mistake of forcing the change of the blowing winds. When the winds of change blow in the area of church leadership, stay with the Book of God. It will set you free.

Membership Winds

Etiquettes

At the very heart of this living organism known as the church, are people the Bible identifies as members (I Corinthians 12:12-24). Every member is important to the functionality and survival of the body (I Corinthians 12:23-24). If one were to remove the members, there would be no such thing as the church. Church membership is also implied in the use of this metaphor of the Body of Christ. The church then is not a physical place or building where corporate gatherings take place. In reality, the church comprises people who are identified as members and, therefore, a part of a membership. This called out body of believers over which Christ is head, in which his Spirit dwells, may biblically be identified as members.

Every preacher or minister should understand that these members are people, human beings, and subject to all of the natural human appetites known to mankind. Members bring any number of spiritual challenges into the context of a spiritual community like the church.

They are in every sense of the consideration sheep, and sheep need leadership and protection from bad elements that threaten their survival. When considering the notion of members, ministers are servants to a myriad of mindsets, some of which are not spiritual, yet they are still God's sheep.

Upon a new minister's arrival at a local congregation, members may use several different approaches and may have several different agendas regarding him. Some may advance relationships with motives that are not immediately seen. Be cautious about members who want to help you by finding and personally signing financial responsibility obligations for a place for you to live. Be careful about members who offer to buy you a car of your choice at their expense. Oh yes, there are those members who constantly put large amounts of monies in your hands, allegedly with no strings attached. While at face value these are tremendous offers, they may turn on you for the worst.

These are often-present perfect opportunities for the change of winds to blow. In times when the preacher takes a biblical position with which the member does not agree. The winds of the relationship could change.

In those instances when the preacher may have to address a matter of immorality with the member or someone in their family, the winds of the relationship may change. It is within the realm of possibility that you may have to correct a member who has an erroneous view of scripture too many times, which may also be an occasion for the winds of relationship change to blow.

A wise minister guards himself against these kinds of temptations that look and feel good on the surface, but when things do not go his way, suddenly the winds of change become a new challenge. As much as possible, preachers must remain independent.

Women Winds

Etiquettes

The smartest thing a minister can do is to stay as far away from the women of the congregation as humanly possible. Never put yourself in a position of perceived compromise. Even if it is innocent, perception is often not a respecter of truth. The minister really must avoid the very appearance of evil (I Thessalonians 5:22).

Most preachers are well-dressed, well-spoken, well-groomed, and appear to be a person of power, position, and prominence. This may often be a magnet for attraction for some women. While this is not intended to indict all women, it is nonetheless a warning to avoid, at all costs, women who may have the wrong motives. *Preacher, God may forgive you, but people will never let you forget your indiscretions.*

Over the years I have always thought it to be a prudent practice, while counseling women, to have my wife or another sister present. I never counsel a woman with my office door closed. I have never gotten out of my bed late at night to answer a sister's call of distress without informing my wife of where I was going and who would be there. This type of situation could easily turn into something you never imagined.

In cases where a sister has made an inappropriate advance towards the preacher, you better be careful how you turn her away. Over the years, I have heard too many stories from other ministers about being harsh to a sister who made advances toward him, and when the story was told, she changed the narrative. What I mean by that is she blamed the minister for the advance. Preachers, just be prudent, wise, and sagacious when dealing with the sisters in the church.

As sad as it may be, when the story gets out, sisters who at one point thought to make advances but decided against it, a few older sisters appear to be mad because you did not look their way, and the countless sisters in the church who are heartbroken because they thought better of you, just won't show any mercy. Now the winds of change start to blow over women's issues, a reputation you may never live to shake or live past.

On the other hand, it is not uncommon to have older, mature, knowledgeable sisters in the church who know few bad seeds and are all too happy to give the minister a stern warning about wayward sisters. They are often valuable in balancing your ministry by helping you make the right decisions to avoid this kind of misstep.

Once this wind changes, it may well be the wind to blow you right out the door of ministry and service to the people of God. This is not a challenge to just younger preachers; as a rule, this component will present itself throughout your years in Christian service. Learn to send the right messages to the sisters of the church. It won't hurt to speak publicly and positively about your wife from time to time if you are blessed to have one. Let the church be reminded that you are a family man with family values, and most of all, you are the man of God, therefore, you are spiritual.

A preacher's interactions with the sisters extend beyond the doors of the local congregation where you serve. If you happen to be a preacher who carries the Gospel internationally, be careful that making the wrong decisions concerning your interaction with the sisters while on the road do not end up beating you back home. This as well may cause the winds of your local congregation to change. While on the road, the man of God has to be very careful not to allow himself to be put in a position of compromise. At all costs, protect your integrity and repartition. *Preacher, stay away from the sisters. They are an expense that you cannot afford.*

CHAPTER 8

The Dynamics Of Delegation

Protocols

The work of the church comes with great demands. There is more work to do than most ministers could ever get around to doing. A really bad look and fit for the local church is when she looks and is run like a "mom and pop operation." A mom-and-pop operation is where one or two people do everything. Preachers who are solo workers are prime candidates for heart attacks, bad health, and early burnout.

A smart minister learns early on in the ministry to use the privilege and power of good delegation. Delegation distributes duties, develops disciples, and delivers destinies. It does not take an abundance of discernment to quickly see that the minister cannot and should not try to do all the needed work alone. A dynamic approach to the execution of the many works of the church is the practice of using delegation. After a period of examination, concentration, and evolution any devoted servant should be influenced to use delegation. This really needs to be a standing protocol that serves as an earmark to ministry.

The utilization of sound delegation also aids in performing the works of the church with excellence. Permit me to address the following regarding delegation: namely, delegation defined, delegation demanded, delegation dimensions, delegation delivered, delegation demonstrated, and delegation discipleship.

Delegation Defined

Etiquette

Notwithstanding that delegation in the context of the church may look and feel radically different from the secular world, a good place to start would be with a healthy definition of the word and concept of delegation as seen in our American dictionaries. In the Merriam-Webster's Collegiate Dictionary Tenth Edition pg. 305, delegation is defined as: "the act of empowering to act for another, a group of persons chosen to represent others." (4) Regarding the church, delegation carries with it the idea of selecting qualified people to share in the responsibilities of another, those who are deemed responsible, accountable, and flexible.

Those who fit the model for delegation step into the perfect training ground for future leadership when there is desire and ability. Delegation in the context of the church also carries with it the notion of spiritual maturity or those who have demonstrated a measure of spiritual growth and show a propinquity toward doing well with responsibility.

(4) Merriam-Webster's Collegiate Dictionary Tenth Edition pg. 305

Delegation as Found In Scriptures

Etiquette

It should be noted that delegation may plainly be seen within Holy Scripture. During the life and ministry of our Lord and Savior Jesus Christ, Christ became the very embodiment of delegation. In the Gospel according to John, Jesus acknowledged that He was sent by His Father to do His will, "For I came down from heaven, not to do mine own will, but the will of him that sent me" (John 6:38). This is a clear example of divine delegation as practiced by God the Father. During the earthly ministry of Christ, He chose twelve disciples who would later become apostles and delegated responsibility to them (Matthew 10:1-5).

The Apostle Paul also practiced delegation during his ministry when responding to the problem of neglect of the Grecian widows in the daily ministration (Acts 8:1-6). There is a great example of delegation in the missionary work of Paul, at that time called Saul, when Barnabas, Simeon, Lucius, and Manaen were present, and the Holy Spirit separated Barnabas and Saul to the work they had been called to and were sent out to preach (Acts 13:1-3). This was, in fact, an act of delegation. The Apostle Paul also demonstrated the practice of delegation in the sending of Titus to Crete to set the church in order and ordain elders in every city (Titus 1:5). As the student of the Bible works his way throughout the scriptures, it becomes more and more obvious that delegation is a biblical concept.

In Old Testament times, a dynamic example of delegation may be found as recommended by Jethro, the father-in-law of Moses, and subsequently practiced by Moses as he ministered to the Israelites. In this instance, Jethro convicted the heart of Moses that the practice of attempting to handle the inquiries of the Israelites who desired wisdom and guidance from God was too heavy for one man to carry (Exodus 18:17-18). Jethro's advice to Moses was to use delegation and appoint judges over the people (Exodus 18:21-22). Moses received the counsel given to him by Jethro and did as he recommended; he used delegation (Exodus 18:24).

All of these examples from the lives of Christ, Paul, and Moses are but a sample of the many instances where the use of delegation is prevalent throughout scripture. If delegation was good enough for these great men of God, why would it not be used as a protocol replete with the many etiquettes mentioned in the Bible? Delegation then constitutes wisdom from the Almighty Himself, revealed by the Holy Spirit and recorded for our observation upon the pages of inspiration even until this day.

Delegation is not a practice derived from the corporate world nor from secular America but straight out of the Bible. God delegated to Christ; Christ delegated to the Holy Spirit, the Holy Spirit delegated to the apostles, and the apostles delegated to the disciples and Disciples of Christ. Even today we would be wise to use this great protocol called delegation.

Demands for Delegation

Etiquette

It does not take a Harvard Road Scholar to detect the demand for delegation in the works of the church. A minister has more than he can handle with study, research sermon design and delivery, ministerial counseling, development of programs, ministries, and sitting with other leaders to project the healthy direction of the church. Surely any wise minister may see the need for delegation. The more a congregation develops and grows, so will the needs of that congregation. The minister needs help for the church to meet her fullest potential.

In these days filled with perilous times, the church has much work to do. The local church must utilize every conceivable approach and opportunity to get the gospel out to the masses. These are just a few of the myriad of reasons why there is a demand for the practice of delegation in the local church. Churches are filled with individuals who are willing and able to assist with the missions of the local community--people who may need guidance in unmoving their intended Kingdom purpose. This is yet another reason why the delegation of Kingdom work is a real need. This is an excellent opportunity to develop disciples for Christ, who may gain more exposure and familiarity with the notion of people serving people.

Delegation as a ministry protocol is a perfect way to empower people to use their giftedness to the honor and glory of God. This garners demand.

In many cases, the demands of a growing church may quickly outgrow a leader's ability to meet those demands. One answer to this dilemma is to get more people involved in the grassroots of these ministries. Why not delegate in order to alleviate? I learned a long time ago that I do not have to be the smartest or hardest worker at the table; I just need smart, hard-working people to be at the table. The minister needs the elevation protocol mindset to position the church to become bigger and better in her missions.

The ongoing need for developing new and relevant ministries and programs in the church points to the need for delegation. Nothing is more rewarding than to be in the position to not be the only one on the team that is expected to plan and execute the works of ministry. With this framework of thinking in the forefront of your mind, the minister will be able to identify an untold number of people who will meet this need for delegation.

Learn to collaborate with other church leaders for their input and perspective about potential people to whom responsibilities may be delegated. The objective is to meet the demand for needed delegation. You need as much input and help as possible. Remember, this is not a mom-and-pop operation; it is one for all and all for one.

As you endeavor to meet the demand for delegation, be careful about *"the whosoever will,"* let them come approach. A word of caution: it is easier to involve people than it is to uninvolve them. Delegation works best when people are selected as opposed to people volunteering. Some have desires with no ability. Do not be rash in your desire to meet the demand.

The Dimensions of Delegation

Etiquette

There are a number of sides, slants, or dimensions to the practice of delegation. The mastery needed in delegation is to get the right person for the right job. Some people are good at managing physical things but not good with people. There are those who are good with people but not good at managing physical things. Some do not work well with or over groups of people but do a masterful job if they have a solo assignment. Again, the point is to select the right person for the right responsibility.

As the person navigating the delegation, you must understand that there are many dimensions to working with delegation. Discerning the right time to cheerlead, coach, celebrate or check up on a delegate calls for understanding the difference in these diverse dimensions. At some point in your leadership with people to whom responsibilities have been delegated, you will need to be a cheerleader and push them to excellence.

Still, at other times you may need to coach or instruct those to whom responsibilities have been delegated. In yet another session the need may be to celebrate or compliment the accomplishments of the person to whom you have entrusted delegation. From time to time, you may even need to check or inquire about the status of an assignment. These are simply different dimensions that come with the territory called delegation.

While studying the classic case of delegation embodied in the exchange between Jethro and his son-in-law

Moses, as found in (Exodus 18). I have often asked myself several questions: Was there a reason why some men were to be appointed over thousands, some hundreds, some fifties, and some tens (Exodus 18:21)? Could this be because different men had different abilities? Or perhaps there were some people with greater and lesser questions and concerns?

While the text does not say, we do know that Moses had to determine which men would judge over which numerical groups. This shows differing dimensions engulfed in determining appropriately dispensed delegation. This also means that delegation relegates to some degree of judgment.

Different people have various levels of abilities; not everyone can take on the same measure of delegation. This is a part of the delegation process that calls for carefulness; it is always more fair to appoint someone than it is to have to remove them from a delegated position.

Discipleship Development through Delegation

Etiquette

According to an article written by Robert L. Foster entitled "Discipleship in the New Testament" (5) Foster wrote: "The word "disciple" appears in the New Testament 261 times in the gospels and the book of Acts. What did it mean to be a disciple? In the ancient Hellenistic world, a disciple was a pupil or learner of a great teacher. Direct contact with the great teacher was not a prerequisite to following their teaching."

(5) Discipleship in the New Testament by Robert L. Foster published by the Society of Biblical Literature

In Vines Expository Dictionary of Old and New Testament Words by W. E. Vines Pg. 308, (6) Vines wrote lit., a learner (from manthano, to learn, from a root math -, indicating thought accomplished by endeavor), in contrast to didaskalos, a teacher; hence it denotes one who follows one's teaching, as the disciple John (Matthew 9:14).

The noun form occurs about 260 times; at least 230 times, the word "disciple" occurs in the four gospels, and the remaining 28 times in Acts. On the other hand, the English word "disciple" comes from the late Latin word for "pual."

In the article "Discipleship in the New Testament", (6) Foster wrote:

"The first disciples in the gospels actually devoted themselves to the way of life taught by John the Baptist. The gospel of John depicts this time of discipleship as rather short-lived since John the Baptist understood his own work as in part a preparation for the coming of Jesus. According to the gospels, John the Baptist saw Jesus as someone so much greater than himself that he felt unworthy to even untie the sandals on Jesus' feet (John 1:27; Matt. 3:11; Mark 1:7; Luke 3:16).

When Jesus comes on the scene John immediately points his disciples to Jesus, whom the disciples address as "Rabbi," ("teacher;" John 1:35-39). When John's disciples express concern over the fact that Jesus' disciples start to outnumber John's, John encourages them to embrace this turn of events as devotion to his own teaching about his relationship with Jesus. John portrays himself in the story as one who attends to the needs of the bridegroom at a wedding and rejoices when all the attention turns toward the bridegroom.

(6) W. E. Vines Expository Dictionary of the Old and New Testament pg. 308

(7) Discipleship in the New Testament by Robert L. Foster Society of Biblical Literature

With a casual look at the New Testament Gospels and the Book of Acts, it becomes clear that discipleship is a world of learning and following. The learning and following are enjoyed under an identifiable teacher who has assignments and instructions to be followed. In the world of delegation, this would be the person delegating any duties to be regarded by a disciple. This becomes the perfect time to impress upon the person or persons accepting the task of delegation to learn the power of being a follower. If they are taught to follow Christ, they can also be taught to follow the assignments delegated. There is something to be said about

CHAPTER 9

Hats Worn By the Church

Protocols

It was not long after I graduated from school with my first undergraduate degree that I suddenly realized that while I had been trained in the Bible from Genesis to Revelation, I had no training in matters of church administration; the many shades of church business. As a result, I learned several lessons the hard way. I was forced to learn the business of the church while in the trenches.

What You Don't Know Will Hinder You

Etiquettes

This was not just about preaching, teaching, and counseling the members; this was also about church business. The fact of the matter is that the church wears a number of different hats; hats that often the leaders and members of the local church do not understand. The lack of proper understanding of the varied hats worn by the church can hurt you.

The first and foremost hat worn by the church is the spiritual hat--the hat commanded by God, who created the church. Whatever God mandates, He regulates. The second hat, a hat forced on the church by the times in which we live, is the civil hat. This has to do with the notion of a church being a nonprofit (501) c3 entity. And last of all, there is the practical hat, a balance of the spiritual and civil hats worn in harmony. Let's take some much-needed time to explore the varied hats the church wears.

The Spiritual Hat Worn By the Church

Etiquettes

The notion here of wearing a hat is in a preverbal sense. Without question, the most important hat that the church must wear is its spiritual hat. In this regard, the Word of God must be our final source of authority in all matters of faith and practice (2 Peter 1:3). The church has no right to exist if it is not aiming to fulfill the church's missions as taught in the Holy Scriptures. It is, namely, preaching the Gospel of Jesus Christ to make disciples of men (Matthew 28:19-20); engaging in acts of benevolence (Galatians 6:10); and finally, works of edification, or upbuilding of existing members of the Body of Christ (Ephesians 4:11-12; I Corinthians 14:26).

This constitutes the spiritual hat of the church. Everything done directly or indirectly on the agenda of the church should seek to wear this spiritual hat. After all, the church is not a secular or artificial institution; it is a spiritual living organism driven by a spiritual mission. Therefore, the church does not look to the world for guidance; it seeks its creator, God Almighty. The idea of being spiritual denotes one following the revelations revealed by God's Holy Spirit (I Corinthians 2:9-13).

If she is the church of the living God (I Timothy 3:15), as seen in the Holy Scriptures, she must be run according to the Word of God. This is the lead hat worn by the local church, especially concerning the governance of the local church. In other words, the local church is to follow the apostolic pattern seen in the Bible as to how the church is governed.

The New Testament Bible is replete with apostolic examples of how the church functions (Acts 20:28). These apostolic patterns take precedence when considering all matters of faith and practice. It determines, for all concerned, when, how, and where spiritual decisions are made to direct the church.

While there seems to be a growing trend to gravitate away from the Biblical model in terms of who plans and executes the direction of the people of God based on the Bible, it becomes apparent that the church needs to be better educated regarding her obligation to wear this lead or primary hat. Given wearing this spiritual hat, the local church is not a majority rule or majority consensus-driven animal. It is not run by a board of trustees. Nor is the church, as viewed in the Bible, governed like a secular corporation operating under the direction of a board of directors or select leadership forum that reports decisions to its constituents at an annual meeting. Instead, the church of Christ as seen in the Bible is a theocracy, or maybe it is better to say a monarchical one-man rule, and that one man is Jesus Christ (Ephesians 1:22).

In the early 1980s, a hotbed issue among many congregations was the issue of the rightful role of a board of trustees. Many thought that because churches in great numbers began to incorporate, this innately made trustees leaders in the church, making all the decisions concerning the spiritual direction of the church. Needless to say, this was the wrong hat to wear when providing leadership to the local church. The church is a called-out body of believers, over which Christ is head, in which is Holy Spirit dwells. It is not a for-profit business.

It is true; what you do not know will hurt you. It is a grievous error to lead any church to think that you can conduct the business of God without the Book of God. Too many instances now occur when the men selected come together to provide spiritual direction for the local church, who have little or no knowledge about the Bible. This opens the door for leadership models that are contrary to biblical examples. The lead hat is worn by God and must be followed by the people of God.

The Civil Hat Worn By the Church

Etiquettes

The need for the church to wear the civil hat may very well be one of the most misunderstood issues of our modern times. Over the years, more and more churches have incorporated as non-profit entities. Some have misunderstood the fact that churches are not required by federal, state, or local law to incorporate. The more informed about these matters have elected to incorporate it as a matter of expediency rather than a legal requirement. While it is completely understandable that the matter of liability is ever at the forefront of all minds concerned with the church's well-being, this is not a stand-alone reason for incorporation and does not innately constitute the right of any board of trustees to provide spiritual leadership to the local church. Spiritual leadership is not their hat to wear.

There are a couple of important matters that need to be considered here with respect to whether or not to incorporate. As a rule, church leaders are concerned about the church's tax-exempt status and therefore feel they must incorporate it. With respect to the tax-exempt status of not-for-profit churches, according to the I.R.C. Section 501(c) (3). One finds the following:

Automatic Exemption for Churches:

Churches that meet the requirements of IRC Section 501(c) (3) are automatically considered tax-exempt and are not required to apply for and obtain recognition of tax-exempt status from the IRS.

Although there is no requirement to do so, many churches seek recognition of tax-exempt status from the IRS because this recognition assures church leaders, members, and contributors that the church is recognized as exempt and qualifies for related tax benefits. For example, contributors to a church that has been recognized as tax-exempt would know that their contributions generally are tax-deductible.

"Churches and religious organizations, like many other charitable organizations, qualify for exemption from federal income tax under IRC Section 501(c) (3) and are generally eligible to receive tax-deductible contributions. To qualify for tax-exempt status, the organization must meet the following requirements (covered in greater detail throughout this publication):

- The organization must be organized and operated exclusively for religious, educational, scientific, or other charitable purposes;

- Net earnings may not inure to the benefit of any private individual or shareholder;

- No substantial part of its activity may be attempting to influence legislation;
- The organization may not intervene in political campaigns;
- The organization's purposes and activities may not be illegal or violate fundamental public policy. (8)

With this in mind, churches do not have to incorporate in order to be viewed by the I.R.S. as tax-exempt. Many churches do not understand that this is a judgment made based on expediency and not a legal requirement."

(8) Publication 1828 (Rev. 8-2015) Catalog number 21096G /department of The Treasury Internal Revenue Service **www.irs.gov**

The issue of incorporation by the local church is another matter that must be probed when considering a proper understanding of the civil hat worn by the church. While the Bible commands the people of God to respect the civil government (Romans 13:1-4), the government never takes the lead in the Kingdom of God. Churches are not required to be incorporated for the purposes of providing spiritual leadership, let alone establishing rules and regulations designed to exercise oversight.

The foremost rationale for church incorporation is to avoid the exposures that come with personal liability. In so doing, the incorporated entity must have a board of directors, trustees, and corporate officers (president, treasurer, and secretary). The trustees simply hold the assets of the church in trust. They are not individual owners or shareholders of the church's real estate or monies.

In an article entitled, "Incorporating Your Church: Why and How," released by Brotherhood Mutual, (a reputable and widely used insurance company to a large number of churches across the nation), it is stated: "When an organization becomes incorporated, that means it legally holds the same rights and responsibilities as an individual.

There are many reasons why churches and other ministries should consider incorporation. The most important is to protect individual members from personal liability associated with the negligent actions of fellow members." (9)

The article further states: "Incorporation is enacted at the state level. In most states, the Secretary of State's office handles incorporation procedures. Many states post incorporation paperwork on their official Web sites, which makes incorporation filings more convenient.

The first step to take when incorporating a church is to contact an attorney who is familiar with not-for-profit laws in your state. The attorney will prepare a document known as the Articles of Incorporation. Several standard points are included in this document, such as the church's corporate name. In most states, the Secretary of State's office will do a corporate name search for a small fee to make sure the name does not already exist.

Once the basics are established, the ministry will want to work with its attorney to develop a statement of organizational purpose. Nonprofit organizations (like churches) must clarify that their purposes are strictly charitable and, in the case of a church or other ministry, religious in nature.

After the statement of purpose is established, the procedure of organizational operation must be defined. This is done through a separate document, most commonly referred to as bylaws. For more information about bylaws, see this article on bylaws." (10)

(9) (10) Sources are courtesy of Christianity Today International/Your Church magazine, November/December 1999, Vol. 45, No. 6, Page 10.

None of the above leads to an understanding that this civil hat in some way gives the board of directors, trustees, or other incorporated officers the right to neglect the Word of God and usurp the authority of spiritual leadership.

The Hat of Balance

Etiquette

The hat of balance, or the balanced hat, is selected and worn with respect to its proper place. In this regard, the church wears the spiritual hat in all matters having to do with spiritual governance, works, and missions, as well as all other spiritual considerations concerning the Kingdom agenda. It is unthinkable that a board of directors, trustees, and corporate officers would ignore the Word of God concerning church governance and hire and fire ministers, and reject needed and plausible ministries of the church just because they see themselves as corporate leaders. May I remind you that there are no corporate leaders in the Bible? These positions come along with the civil hat and must be encouraged to remain in their proper place.

This demands balance, as the two hats work together from their respective and rightful places to advance the church's missions. The education of leaders and members concerning these two hats is paramount. This is, in part, the answer to helping the church remain spiritually healthy, functional, and growing numerically. If the church does not enjoy this much-needed education, churches will continue to splinter and stifle because of misinformation and lack of knowledge concerning these unavoidable hats.

Neither of these hats may be ignored, as they are both needed for the betterment of the cause of Christ. It is clarity, truth, and reality that constitute salvation in this matter. Balance is the order of the day. People cannot do what they do not know. It takes courage and a real commitment to the ways of God to stand your ground about the rightful places of these hats, yet it is the preacher's responsibility to set the church in order, and this falls under his calling by God (Titus 1:5).

Over the years, I have seen a number of great ministries and churches fall apart, some even split, as a result of a failure to be knowledgeable about these hats respectively. The Bible must retain the lead, and at the same time, civil rules must be followed in instances where they do not contradict the commands of God. This is the magic of balance between man and God.

CHAPTER 10

The Honor of Hosting

Protocol

One of the distinct honors of local ministry is that of hosting local, regional, and national church events, including gospel revivals, conferences, lectureships, workshops, and the like. Nevertheless, there are a number of challenges that surface while attempting to enjoy the honor of hosting. The primary objective of hosting should be doing it with distinctive excellence. The man of God always wants to make God and the church look good by how they handle God's business.

Whether you elect to see it this way or not, your creditability and reputation are at stake, let alone the creditability and reputation of the church where you serve. Excellence must become your driving motivation as a good host. Let's examine a few suggested etiquettes that hopefully will help you execute the art of hosting with excellence. Remember that the ability to host should be considered an honor. What makes this an honor is the opportunity to stand out as an example, demonstrating the fact that we serve a God of excellence, and every effort hosted by the church holds the privilege of honoring Him with excellence.

The Budget Etiquettes

A major consideration with respect to hosting any event is the financial budget. It is simply inconceivable to attempt to host an event without the needed finances. To a great extent, what a church can and cannot do relegates to financial ability. It is not recommended to wing your way through trying to pull off a big congregational-hosted event, knowing full well that the church does not have the money. This is a train wreck waiting to happen.

Developing a projected budget to facilitate your proposed event is the only way to go. All things are about the budget. Beware of financially overextending yourself, understanding that the event may be too costly. Stay within your budget from start to finish. Be mindful of all the varied components that are needed to provide you with the bottom-line cost projections required to carry out the event with excellence. Never depend on the understanding and benevolent spirit of vendors, guests, or any other components that go into the uptake of your proposed event. If the church cannot afford it, it is wise not to attempt it.

Several considerations must be at the forefront of a host's mind. Namely, are you trying to do too much? A sample case in point: You are hosting a revival meeting. Finances are tight, yet you want to invite a 12-member choral group. You are now confronted with transportation costs, hotel costs, food, and a stipend, on top of what must be done to care for the guest minister who has been invited to conduct the revival.

Already your budget is in potential trouble. Your church is setting itself up for failure. Set a projected budget and be realistic about dispensing expenditures. Remember: it is all about the budget.

Invitation

Etiquettes

The next important step is selecting the right person or persons to guest appear at your planned event. Preacher, this is not the time to pay favors to those who, in the past, have invited you to participate in an event hosted by them. This is not the time to play trade-off; in other words, "You come and preach for me, and then I will come and preach for you." The church wants to select the best person for the job, someone with a proven track record for faring well at the appointed task.

Consider sending them a formal letter of invitation replete with all the needed particulars to help them determine whether they feel comfortable accepting the invitation. Such a letter of invitation should include the day, date, and times of the event. The revealing of the event thematic, if applicable, what the church will cover concerning expenses like round trip airfare, baggage, hotel, daily transportation to and from the event, food, stipend, reimbursement for out-of-pocket expenses incurred, and the like should also be spelled out. Often if the invited guest is married, if it is budget-friendly, you can make the offer to cover the expenses of bringing their spouse along on the trip.

The idea is to cover as much as possible in the letter of invitation as deemed relevant. Preacher, put it in print. This covers the church and the invited guest in terms of expectations.

In these modern times, it has become expected to communicate a letter of invitation via email, as opposed to the old-school physical letter. This is also an approach to reach out to an invited guest with the needed details and terms of a speaking engagement. The point of this etiquette is to pursue excellence during the invitation stage with clarity and transparency.

The Big Secret

Etiquettes

As ministers of the gospel of our Lord Jesus Christ, we are servants (Romans 1:1), teachers (Matthew 28:19-20), and preachers (2 Timothy 4:1) of the Word of God. It is not a gospel preacher's primary objective or motive to preach just for the sake of earning money. If making money is your motivation, you may want to find another line of work. At the same time, the Bible is clear that those who preach the gospel live of the gospel (I Corinthians 9:14).

In the minister's travels and works, you will eventually run into what is called by some "The Big Secret." That's when you are invited to be a guest speaker at a church event, and all the details surrounding the event are openly shared, with the exception of compensation. The conversation or letter of invitation seems to stop short of the mention of money. In many of these instances, the invited minister will not know if there is compensation or how much the compensation amount is until the event is over and you are ready to return home. It just feels like one big secret.

Now let's enjoy a moment of honesty: is it fair to invite a guest speaker to leave home, duties, responsibilities, and family to be a guest at a church's event without any indication whatsoever as to whether there will be any compensation associated with the invitation? Is it really ethical, moral, or spiritual to be all right with your invited speaker spending his own monies for cleaning clothing, transportation to the airport, feeding himself while making the mad dash to catch a plane, putting their own credit card up at the hotel for possible incidentals, without any notions as to if there will be any compensation involved at all? "Who goes to war at his own charges" (I Corinthians 9:7)? Or what happened to "Muzzle not the mouth of the ox that treadeth out the corn" (I Corinthians 9:9)? The big secret is a very poor etiquette by which to operate.

Tell the person invited what may be expected in terms of possible compensation and let them be the judge if this is doable for them. No secrets! As a part of the letter of invitation, or for that matter in an initial phone call, these kinds of particulars ought to be spelled out. As an invited guest, churches have asked me over the years, "How much do you charge to come and preach?" In 45 years of preaching and travel, I have never ever made it a practice to put a monetary amount on preaching the gospel. As far as I am concerned, that's God's business. He will provide. Yet ministers deserve to know what they are up against when considering an invitation to be at your church event.

Post-Pandemic Policies

Etiquettes

In recent years, the works of the church have taken on a new look as churches worldwide have had to reinvent and re-think how she does ministry. During the time frame of the global pandemic 2020-2023, an untold number of churches were forced to close their doors to in-person services. During this same period of time, congregations had to figure out how to keep doing ministry and ways that did not violate clear scriptural teachings to provide virtual formats by which Christians could worship from their respective spaces. Suddenly the world of pre-recording services became the popular way to go. In late March of 2020, so many churches were online (via Facebook and Zoom) that the internet crashed because it could not hold the virtual demand.

To date, as churches have started to reopen to in-person services, there remains a large number of pre-pandemic members of churches who have not returned to in-person services. Some have even taken the position that many of them will never return to the in-person service experience again. When it is all said and done, it seems that the virtual world for the church is here to stay, at least in some capacity or another. Several matters are time worthy of our consideration concerning recommended etiquettes to help aid the church in responding with excellence to the pseudo demand for the virtual animal.

Inviting a minister or speaker to provide a pre-recorded sermon, lecture, or workshop post-pandemic is much more involved than meets the eye. I have witnessed a number of instances when individuals have been requested to participate in a sermonic presentation or a series of messages and offered no financial compensation or relief at all. Yet that individual has the task of securing a person to video record the message or messages, edit them, and electronically send them to the host destination.

More often than not, these are not free services to a speaker. Just because a speaker is not in person does not mean the work effort is not worthy of some consideration of compensation. Who compensates the production team (sound person, videographer, editor)? Churches must consider being fair in the context of requesting a speaker to pre-record messages and send them to the host church, in addition to consideration of the presenter. I suppose this is a nice way of saying that churches in this post-pandemic period should consider giving a stipend to the speaker that would allow a portion for their production team to be compensated as well. Pre-recorded messages are an expense to your invited speaker. Is it fair for that speaker to bear the burden of expense because you invited them to participate in your event?

In fact, the average church will invest less money in a virtually hosted event than spending the money to bring in an in-person speaker. What is currently being experienced by many speakers in great demand is just unethical and impartial; maybe a better word is unfair. In the context of a post-pandemic period, the church must rethink how she treats ministers and their respective contributions to the Kingdom agenda.

CHAPTER 11

The Art of Officiating

Protocol

Over the years, it has been my good fortune to have attended many corporate services, funerals, weddings, national, regional, and local lectureships, gospel concerts, and more. However, what has become a matter of fascination to me is what appears to be an unbelievable number of ministers and other church leaders that do not seem to understand the art of officiating these kinds of services. Showing up to events at the last minute, wearing inappropriate attire, being unprepared for their presentation, sometimes using insulting language, a public display of a lack of compassion and sensitivity toward grieving families, and often presenting the wrong kind of message to the wrong audience all demonstrate a lack of excellence.

There is an art to officiating. As the years have gone by, I am more and more grateful that I came up under mature and experienced ministers and other church leaders who were men of profound principles concerning the seriousness of this art. More training should be offered to those who attempt to serve in these capacities. After all, doing what you do not know is not easy. I am convinced that many of these good men mean no offense; they have not had the training and exposure to the art. While a youngster in the church, there was constant training for service classes where we learned how to officiate over the Lord's Table, contribute, lead public prayer, read scripture, and even lead a song service. It is interesting that we often do not have this training for ministers and church leaders in what is needed to officiate any number of services with excellence.

Officiating Funerals

Etiquette

When a family calls upon a minister or church leader to officiate a funeral service of a cherished loved one, a memorial service, or a graveside service, the minister must think about what he will say. Much of the attention will be on the message and movement of the minister or church leader officiating. He will be the lead person to set the tone of the service. When the minister has been asked to officiate these services, consider whether the deceased was a Christian or non-Christian, a faithful or unfaithful attender to services. Is this person being eulogized a loved one of a church member where you preach? All of this and more will impact your intended declarations.

Your primary responsibility is to declare a Word from the Lord. While the service may be designed to remember the life and legacy of the departed, your focus for declaration is aimed at those yet in the land of the living. This is a prime opportunity to tell men and women about salvation and the saving love of Christ; the direction in which your address must be built is the Gospel. At all costs, avoid undue judgments about perceived lousy family dynamics.

Several years ago, I attended a home-going service at a small Tennessee church. The minister rose to deliver his message and elected to use this time to rebuke the children of the deceased because of their public lamenting and grieving over their loss. He told the family they had no right to cry now because they did not seem to care about him when he was alive. This was highly inappropriate, disrespectful, and out of character for an officiating man of God who was supposed to preach the Gospel, comfort the family, and speak well of the departed.

Considering your declaration, avoid making unscriptural remarks and observations like, "Your loved one's body is gone, but you can still speak to their spirit."

That is not what James said in (James 2:25); the soul is gone, gone to a place where they can no longer hear them. So, Minister, this is misguided comfort because it does not tell the Bible's truth. Preachers, avoid attempts to justify the death of a person who overdosed on drugs and has died because of it by saying, "This is God's will. He never makes a mistake." The art of officiating suggests that you are insightful enough to lift the family, not challenge them theologically with misguided applications. A smart officiant never underestimates the informedness of his audience. Some people know better.

Learn to be timely when officiating any service: start on time and end on time. As an officiant, you are the primary person in control of the atmosphere, the spirit, and the feeling of excellence in the air. It does not matter what kind of service you are officiating. Your primary objective is to make God, the church, and yourself look good.

Officiating Weddings

Etiquettes

Without question, one of the greatest joys is the honor of officiating the nuptials of a couple about to spend the rest of their lives together. This is a day they and their families will remember for a lifetime. Requiring premarital counseling before the big day may be a good idea and an excellent place to start to get to know them and help them consider several things that may not have come to their minds. Someone once said that good understanding in the front makes for no misunderstanding in the rear. So, let's approach this with excellence. Ask the couple which colors they plan to wear and color coordinate with them, being careful not to overshadow the bride or groom's attire. Before the wedding day, you should know the full names of both the bride and groom and, if needed, learn the pronunciation of difficult family names. Never take a couple by surprise by not going over the details of their intended service.

For instance, is this a double-ring ceremony (both receive rings)? Will they write their vows in addition to the traditional vows? Will there be a candle lighting ceremony, the broom's jumping, or the knot tying? Will the respective mothers receive gifts as a part of the ceremony? Please avail yourself of the opportunity to meet and greet the mothers and fathers of the bride and groom before the ceremony starts, should they be living and present. Also, greet both the bride and the groom and have a word of prayer with them before the service.

Put extra effort into every wedding service to make it unique to that couple. The execution of the ceremony is where the proverbial magic takes place. Explain the respective parts of the service as you go through it. The purpose of the vows, what marriage means to God, and the couple being joined together by God. Explain the symbolism of the wedding rings, the tying of the knot, the unity cup, the unity candle, and any other parts of the service. Finally, explain the role of the person giving the bride away. All of this makes for an extraordinary service, one the couple will never forget. Be a servant to the couple getting married by offering to mail in the wedding license for them after all parties have signed. Do not be in such a hurry to get away after the service; stay and take pictures with them on this memorable occasion.

We live in a time where 50% of all marriages now end in divorce. After the big day's excitement has ended, make yourself available to the couple you have just married in the event they need further counseling or maybe even crisis intervention should things go in the wrong direction early in the marriage. Preacher, great weddings are not born. They are created, and the couple may need you again.

Officiating Corporate Assemblies

Etiquette

There are other services to which a minister or a church leader may be called upon to officiate. When officiating any service, you must consider three things— Declaration, Decorum, and Demeanor. In other words, how you talk, look, and behave. May I remind you that you are a leader and are held to a higher standard than others? You represent God, the church, and yourself.

How to talk, look, and behave should be driven by excellence. You want to talk, look, and behave in a manner that is becoming of a minister of the Gospel of Jesus Christ. While I realize that parts of this are subjective, I am reminded that it is always good, better, and best. You are aiming for the best.

Here are definitional perspectives of what is meant by declaration, decorum, and demeanor. A declaration, according to the Merriam-Webster's Collegiate Dictionary Tenth Edition, means: "The act of declaring: Announcement, a statement made by a party to a legal transaction, not under oath, something that is declared." (17) One of the first and foremost duties of an officiant is as a speaker or one who makes declarations. One should do so with great clarity, exercising carefulness concerning the use of the English language, and speaking with distinctive tone and articulation. These are earmarks of excellence. What people hear is the first impression; some call it commanding the room, and it is all about gaining and keeping people's attention with your speech or declaration.

(17) Merriam-Webster's Collegiate Dictionary Tenth Edition Pg. 299

The second duty of an officiant is that of decorum. The Merriam-Webster's Collegiate Dictionary Tenth Edition says of decorum: "Propriety and good taste in conduct or appearance, orderliness, the conventions of polite behavior." (18) The eyes of your audience are on you; how you conduct yourself speaks to a great extent about your person, who you are. A man of God should always be on his best behavior, projecting the highest moral fiber and character standards. While we live in a time and culture where personal appearance has become subjective, the man of God ought to present with an A-game mentality.

Learn to respect the culture of the people and the place by being perceived as one who speaks, dresses, and conducts oneself appropriately, whatever the occasion. An important part of people's perception of you will be judged by how you dress and talk. It is strange, this pseudo-controversy of our time concerning appropriate dress in the church context, yet no one would wear a bathing suit to a wedding, a bikini swimsuit to a funeral, flip flops to a ski resort. Why all the controversy over what is considered appropriate in a corporate church assembly? It is not uncommon to hear some people say, "Just come as you are. God does not judge the outward appearance. He looks upon the heart." *Ministers should be people who set higher than normal standards for themselves as well as those with whom they work.*

Whether it is a locally hosted revival, gospel concert, lectureship conference, workshop or worship service, the man of God must give great attention to how he talks, looks, and acts and do so with excellence.

(18) Merriam-Webster's Collegiate Dictionary Tenth Edition Pg. 300

The third duty of a minister or church leader with the responsibility of officiating is that of his demeanor. Merriam-Webster's Collegiate Dictionary defines decorum as: "Behavior toward others, outward manner." (19) An officiant must guard himself against all perceived inappropriate behaviors. As ministers of the Gospel of Jesus Christ, all we have is our integrity. Once a man of God loses his integrity it is difficult to regain.

Over the years it has been a matter of amazement to realize that those who lead live in a fishbowl. People watch and listen to virtually everything done and said. Preacher, your behavior speaks to how you are. Avoid jokes that are in bad taste and the appearance of being antagonistic toward others. Steer clear of roaming eyes that seem to be fixed on the sisters. Be cautious about the manner in which you may be called upon to handle difficult people and difficult situations. All of this and more speaks to your demeanor, and if mishandled can earn you a bad reputation.

Leader, your declaration, decorum, and demeanor together are the sum total of how you represent. It does not matter how talented you are in your oratory, homiletical and hermeneutical skills if you set a bad example with how you talk, look, and act. Strive in these characteristics to reach levels of excellence, and your service will bless the lives of those you serve. I pray that more Kingdom servants will have a servant's heart, spirit, and attitude as they develop into the quintessential officiant.

(18) Merriam-Webster's Collegiate Dictionary Tenth Edition Pg. 307

A Word about the Author

Dr. O. J. Shabazz

Meet Dr. O.J. Shabazz, a remarkable figure in the world of ministry. Currently serving as the minister to the Church of Christ in vibrant Harlem, New York City, Dr. Shabazz has made a significant impact on the lives of many over the past 23 years. His passion for sharing the gospel has led to the baptism of over one thousand souls, symbolizing his unwavering commitment to the teachings of Christ.

Beyond his local ministry, Dr. Shabazz is widely recognized as a national evangelist within the Churches of Christ. He has fearlessly preached the gospel in 38 states and five foreign nations, captivating audiences with his insightful biblical exegesis. Known for his church-building expertise and sharp administrative skills, Dr. Shabazz has been instrumental in fostering growth and spiritual development within congregations.

One of Dr. Shabazz's greatest joys lies in his role as a trainer and mentor to aspiring Gospel preachers across the nation. His dedication to equipping the next generation of ministers is evident in the time and effort he invests in their development, ensuring they receive comprehensive guidance and support.

Dr. Shabazz's academic accomplishments are equally impressive. He holds multiple academic degrees, including a Bachelor of Arts in Biblical Studies from the esteemed Memphis School of Preaching in Tennessee and a Bachelor's in Christian Education from the prestigious Midwestern Christian Institute in Mount

Clemens, Michigan. Recognizing his significant contributions to the field of ministry, he was awarded an honorary Doctorate of Divinity from the same institute. Driven by his thirst for knowledge, he pursued a Master's in divinity and a Doctorate in Ministry from the esteemed Southern Institute of Biblical Studies in Indianapolis, Indiana.

Outside of his ministry endeavors, Dr. Shabazz cherishes his role as a devoted husband to L.V.R. Shabazz. Together, they have raised a beautiful family of five children and eagerly anticipate the arrival of their ninth grandchild, with one great-grandchild on the way.

Dr. O.J. Shabazz is a man of faith, a compassionate leader, and a relentless advocate for excellence in ministry. His wealth of experience, academic achievements, and passion for empowering others make him an invaluable asset to the global community of believers. Through his teachings, writings, and unwavering commitment to spreading the gospel, Dr. Shabazz continues to inspire and transform countless lives with the message of Christ's love and grace.

Afterword

I must commend Dr. Shabazz for addressing to topic of "Excellence in Ministry." In a world where the ministry of Jesus is often misrepresented by church leaders, this book is rare and refreshing. It is one I find divinely orchestrated. The book contains information that provides profound training for all theologians!

Dr. Shabazz has the ability to share Biblically authenticated truths that cause ministers and church leaders to surrender to the Supremacy of God. This book brought me to a greater appreciation of my own ministry, while at the same time allowing for introspection and enlightenment.

Dr. Shabazz's courage and commitment to telling the full truth regardless of the popular social constructs that might not align with the divine Word of God is really what sets this book apart.

Dr. Tony E. Roach,
God's Love Bank Program and Curriculum author!

Made in the USA
Columbia, SC
22 August 2023

22007896R00085